The Music of Debussy for Solo Guitar

Yago Santos

The Kenny Hill Signature Anniversary Model guitar cover image is courtesy of Hill Guitar Company.

WWW.MELBAY.COM

Preface

The Music of Debussy for Solo Guitar contains eleven pieces by composer Claude Debussy arranged for solo guitar. Except for "Syrinx", which was conceived as a solo flute piece, all of the pieces herein were originally written for the piano. The chosen pieces represent different periods in the composer's life and compositional style, from the legendary "Clair de lune", to the "Arabesque No. 1" and some of his most famous preludes such as "La fille aux cheveux de lin".

Achille-Claude Debussy (1862 - 1918), was a French composer whose works were a seminal force in the music of the 20th century. He developed a highly original system of harmony and musical structure that expressed in many respects the aspirational ideals of the impressionist and symbolist painters and writers of his time.

Debussy's music marks the first of a series of attacks on the traditional language of the 19th century. He did not believe in the stereotyped harmonic procedures of the 19th century, and indeed, it becomes clear from a study of mid-20th-century music that the earlier harmonic methods were being followed in an arbitrary, academic manner. He rejected the theoretical approach to music. In a conversation with one of his former teachers, he declared, "There is no theory. You merely have to listen. Pleasure is the law."

In a letter of condolence sent to Debussy's widow, Manuel de Falla considered Debussy "The Creator of New Music". From his beginnings, Debussy relied on the classical-romantic tradition to search for harmonic and formal alternatives, diving into the music of non-European cultural circles.

His approach to the symbolist poets gave Debussy the necessary push to embark on an innovative path of sound, both in form and structure as well as harmony and timbre. It was a journey steeped in visual references, similar to the one followed by impressionist painters such as Monet or Renoir at that time. The composer may have been the first in history to become a fully modern-minded artist, joining a community of writers and painters, borrowing ideas and lending them in turn.

Light and color are key concepts in Debussy's musical creation, but it should not be classified under the adjective "impressionist", simplifying and deforming it. Indeed, Debussy always rejected this term as a representation of his musical style.

My interest in the music of Claude Debussy arose during my adolescence, when I was first introduced to his work. His figure and philosophy, as well as his music, have always been a source of inspiration for me. Arranging the music in this book has given me a unique opportunity to delve into his music and discover in-depth, the secrets behind the melodies, harmonies and textures that came to revolutionize the music of the late 19th and early 20th centuries.

For me, Debussy represents the most exciting period in the history of music. He accomplished something that happens very rarely, and not in every lifetime; he brought a new kind of beauty into the world. I find it incredible that he never composed a piece for the guitar; that is why I decided to arrange this collection of some of his most famous pieces. It is important for classical and flamenco guitar players to know his harmonies and his musical concepts as applied to our instrument. I hope you will enjoy them and share them with your audiences.

The music in this book is available on Yago Santos CD titled *Tribute to Claude Debussy* (UPC 8428353760914).

Contents

Arabesque No. 1

Claude Debussy
(1862-1918)
Arranger - Yago Santos

Andante con moto

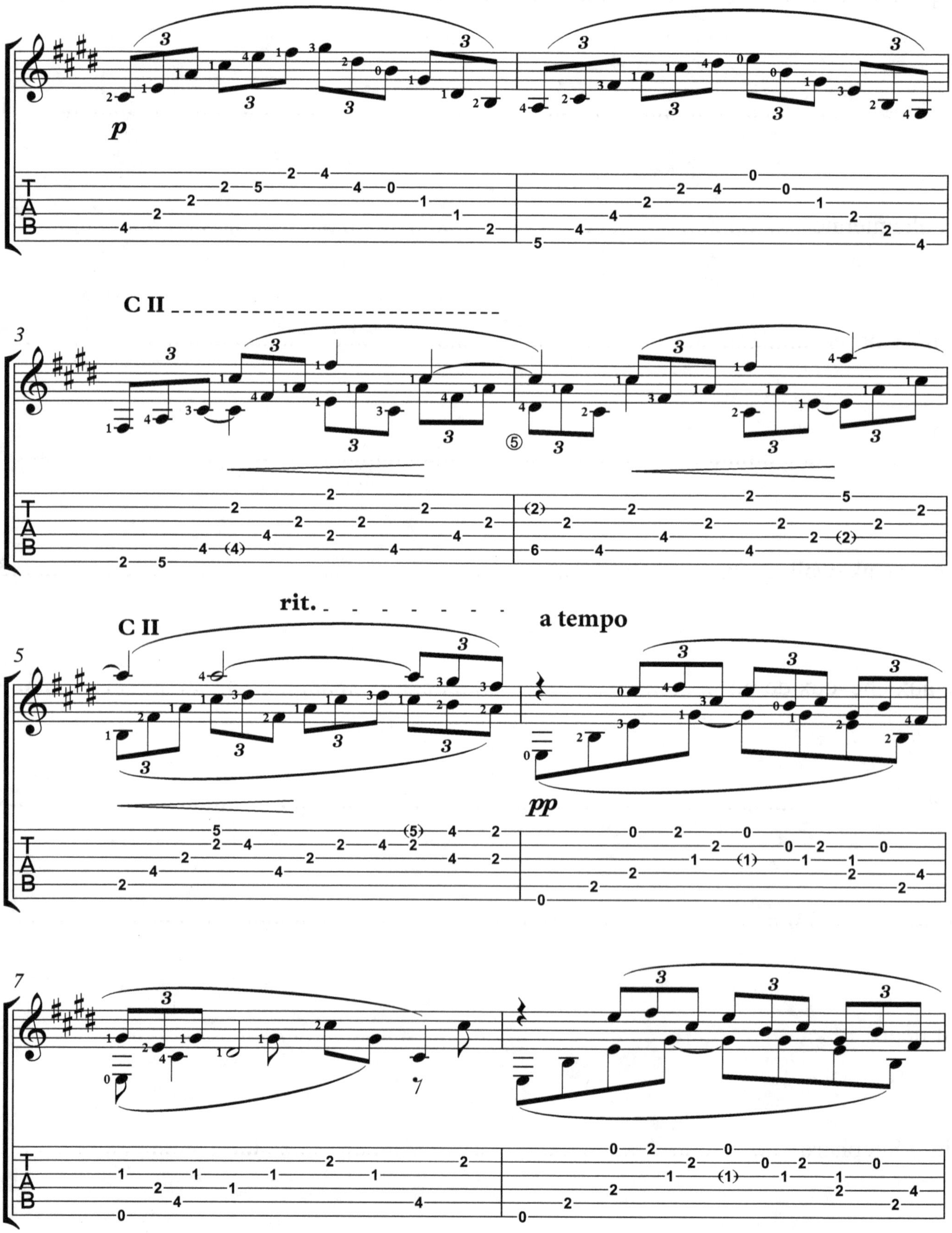

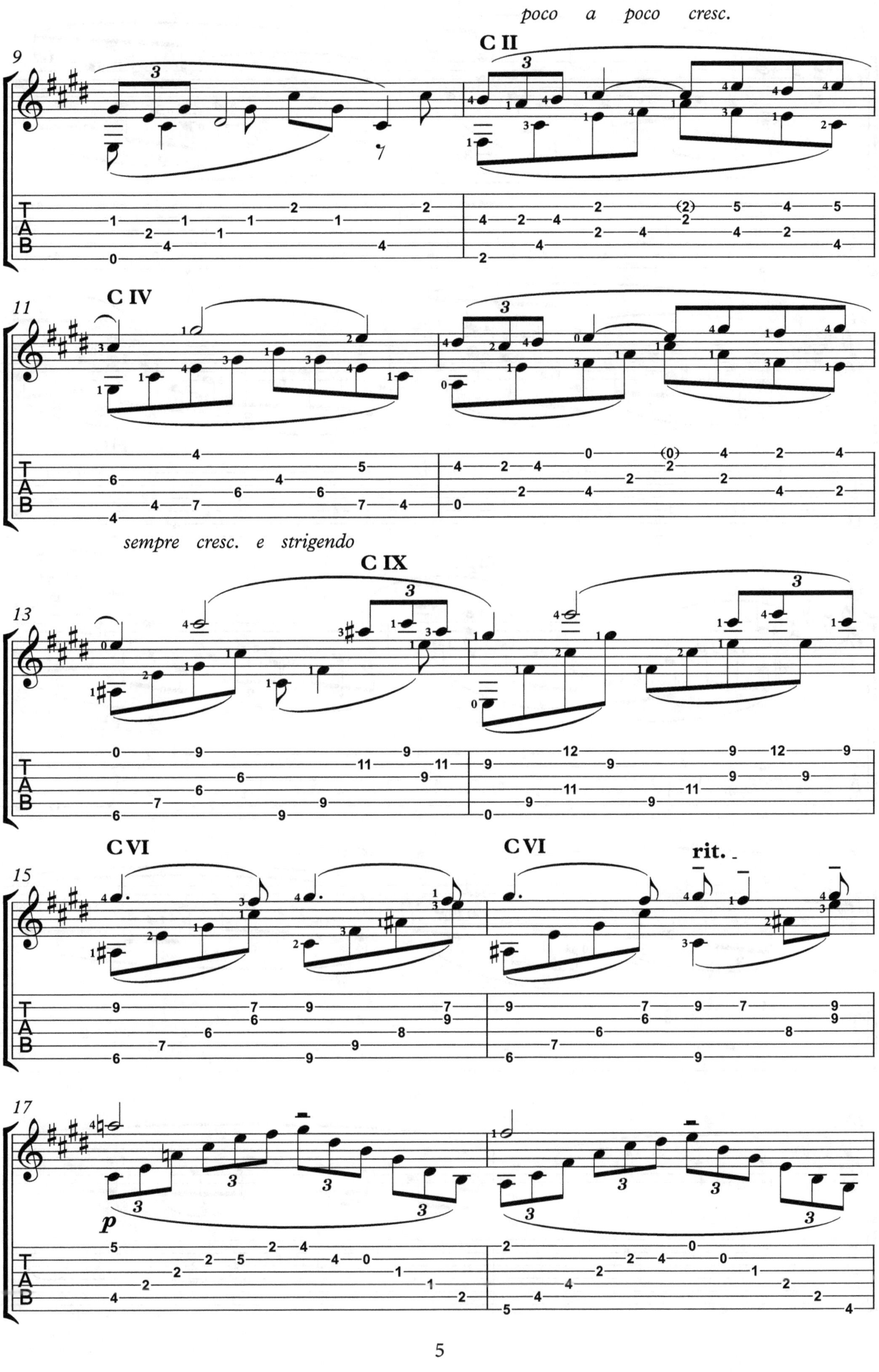
poco a poco cresc.
C II
C IV
sempre cresc. e strigendo
C IX
C VI
C VI
rit.
p

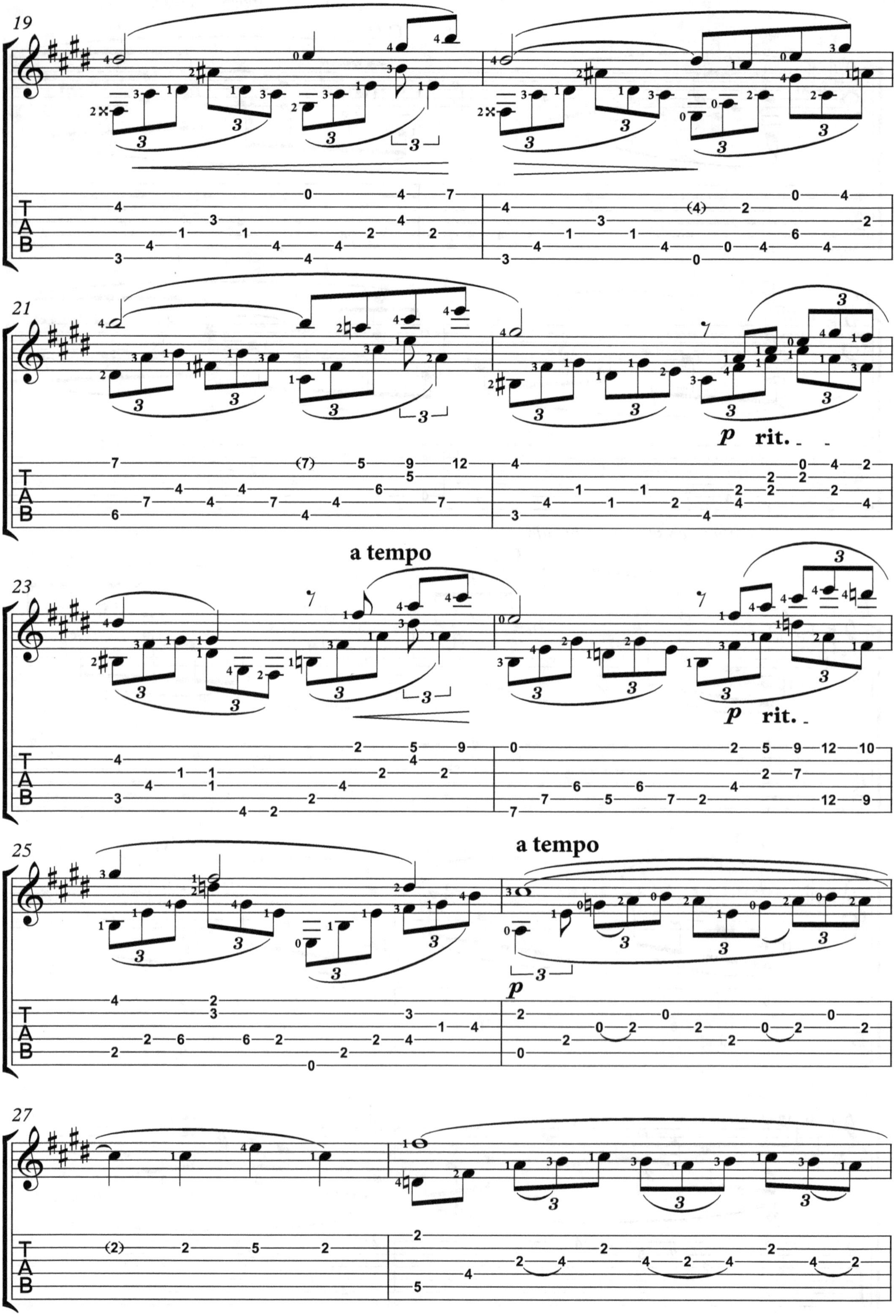
19
21
p rit.
a tempo
23
p rit.
25
a tempo
p
27

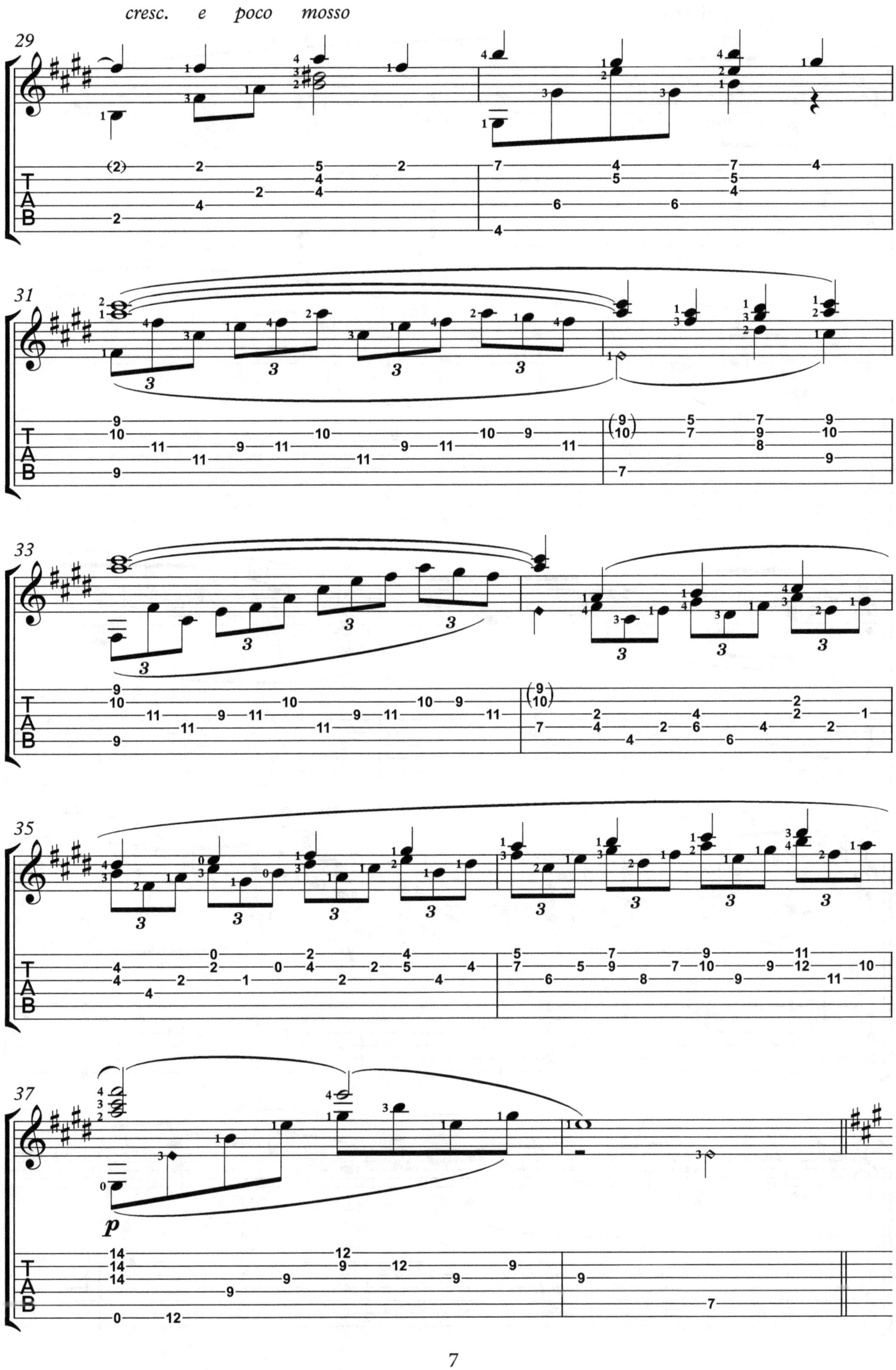
cresc. e poco mosso
p

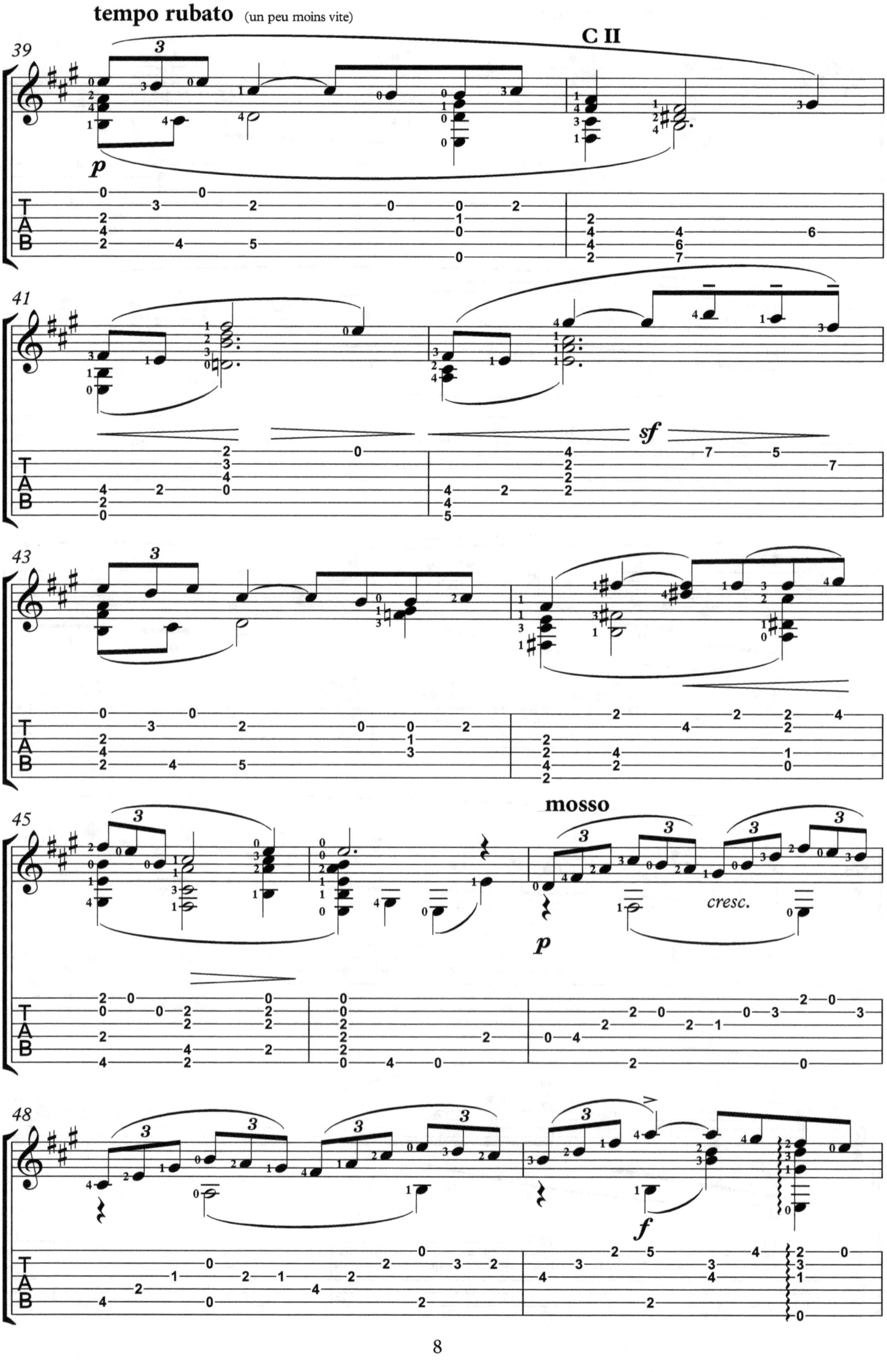
tempo rubato (un peu moins vite)
C II
p
sf
mosso
p
cresc.
f

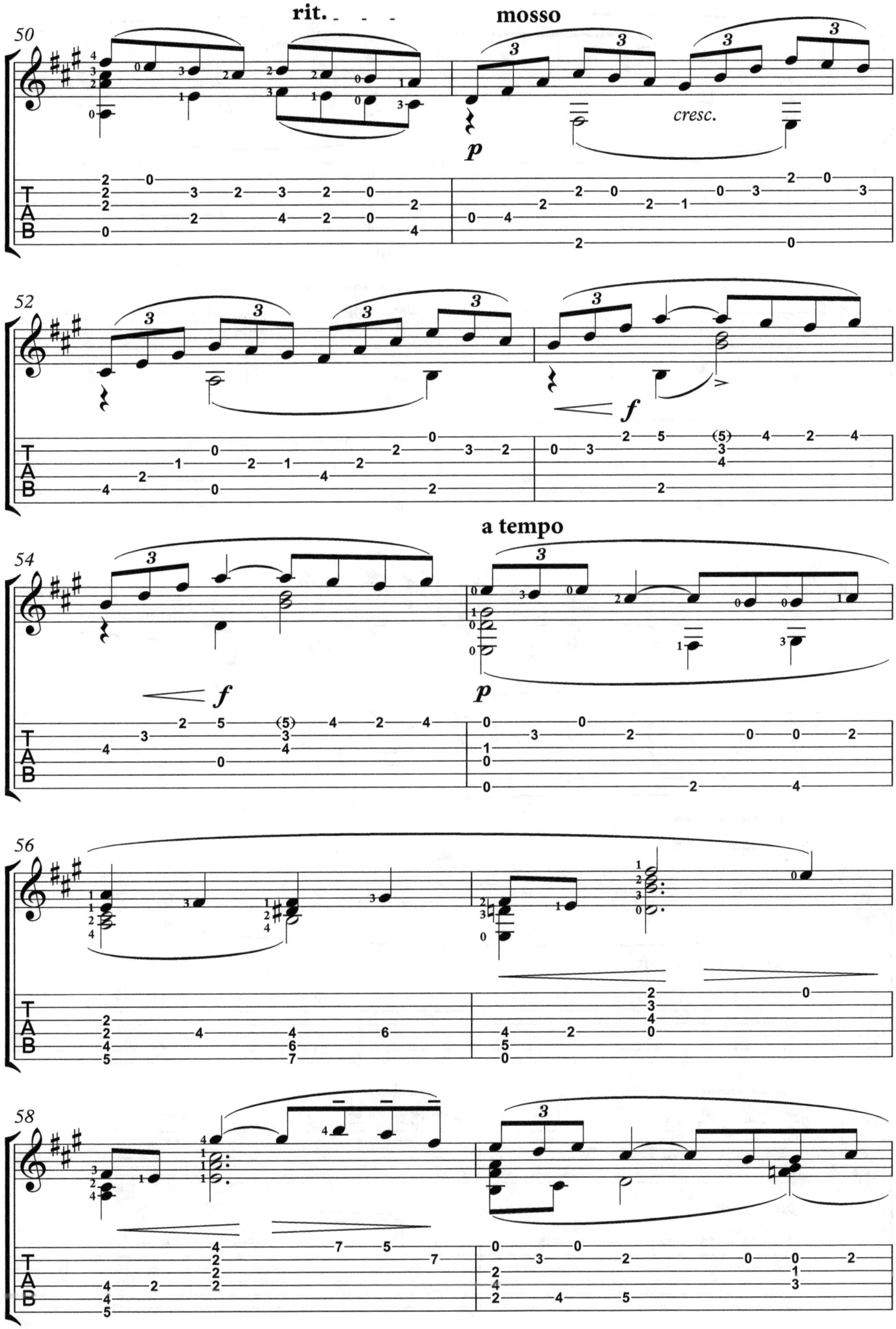
rit.
mosso
cresc.
a tempo

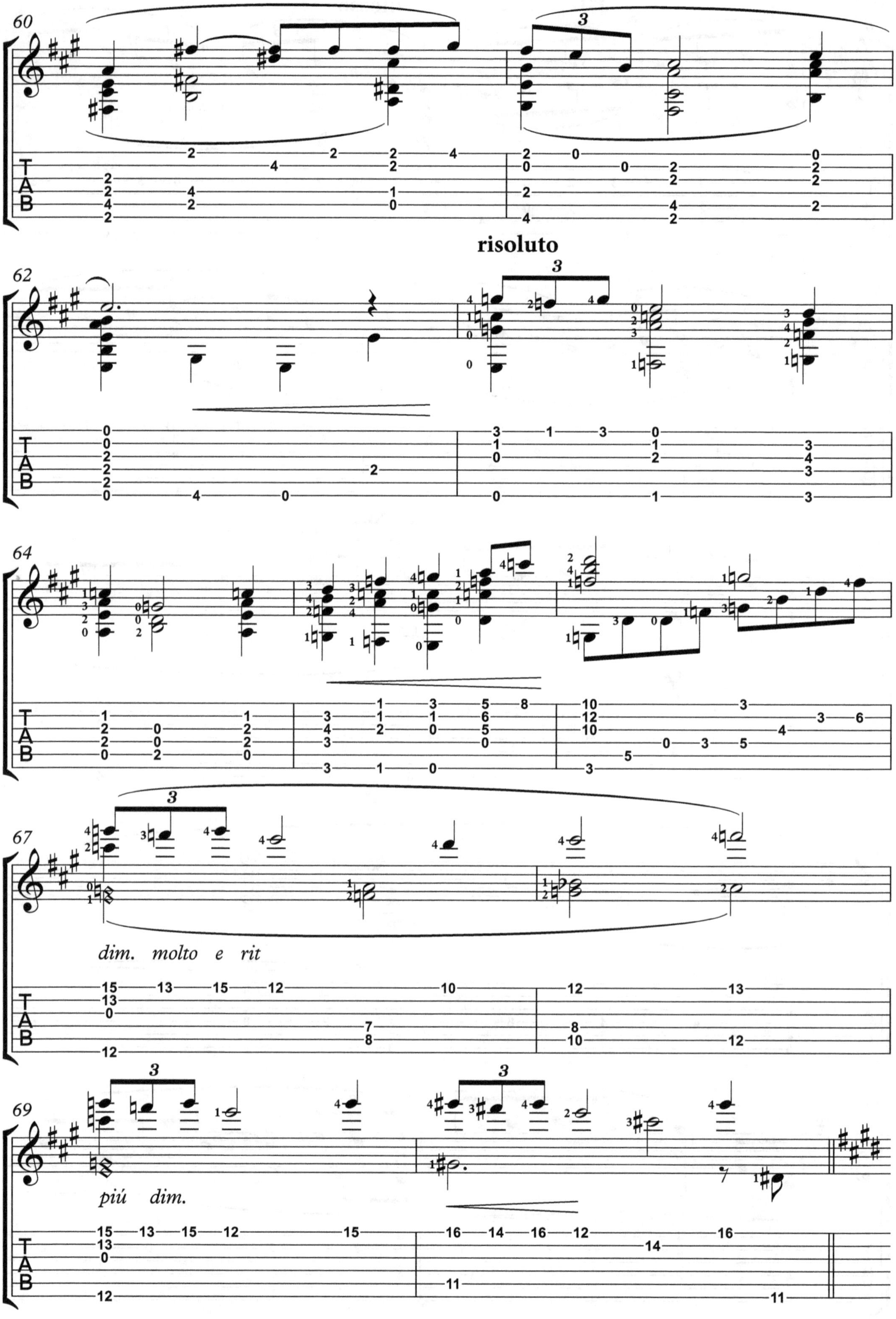
risoluto
dim. molto e rit
piú dim.

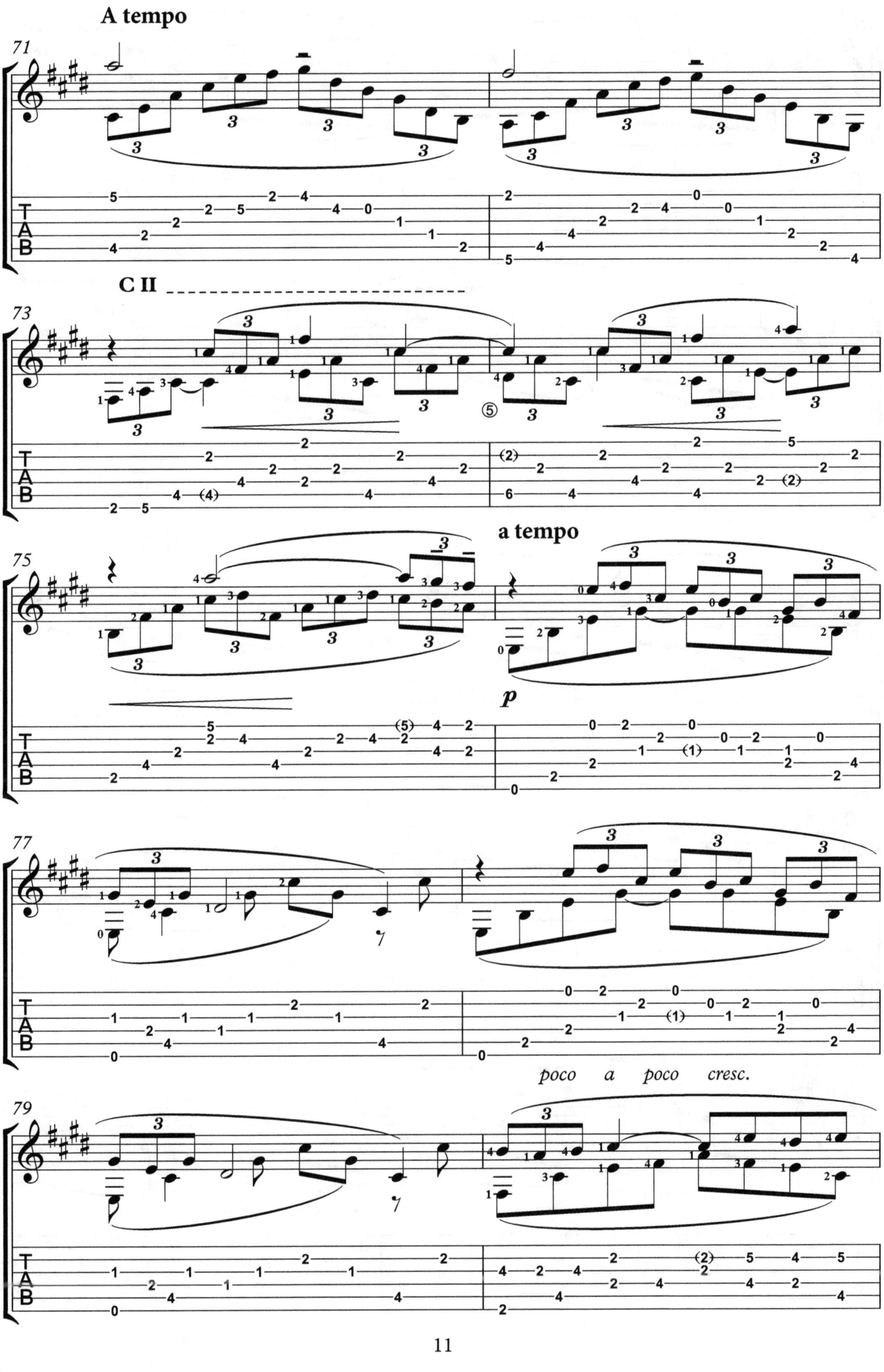
A tempo
C II
a tempo
p
poco a poco cresc.

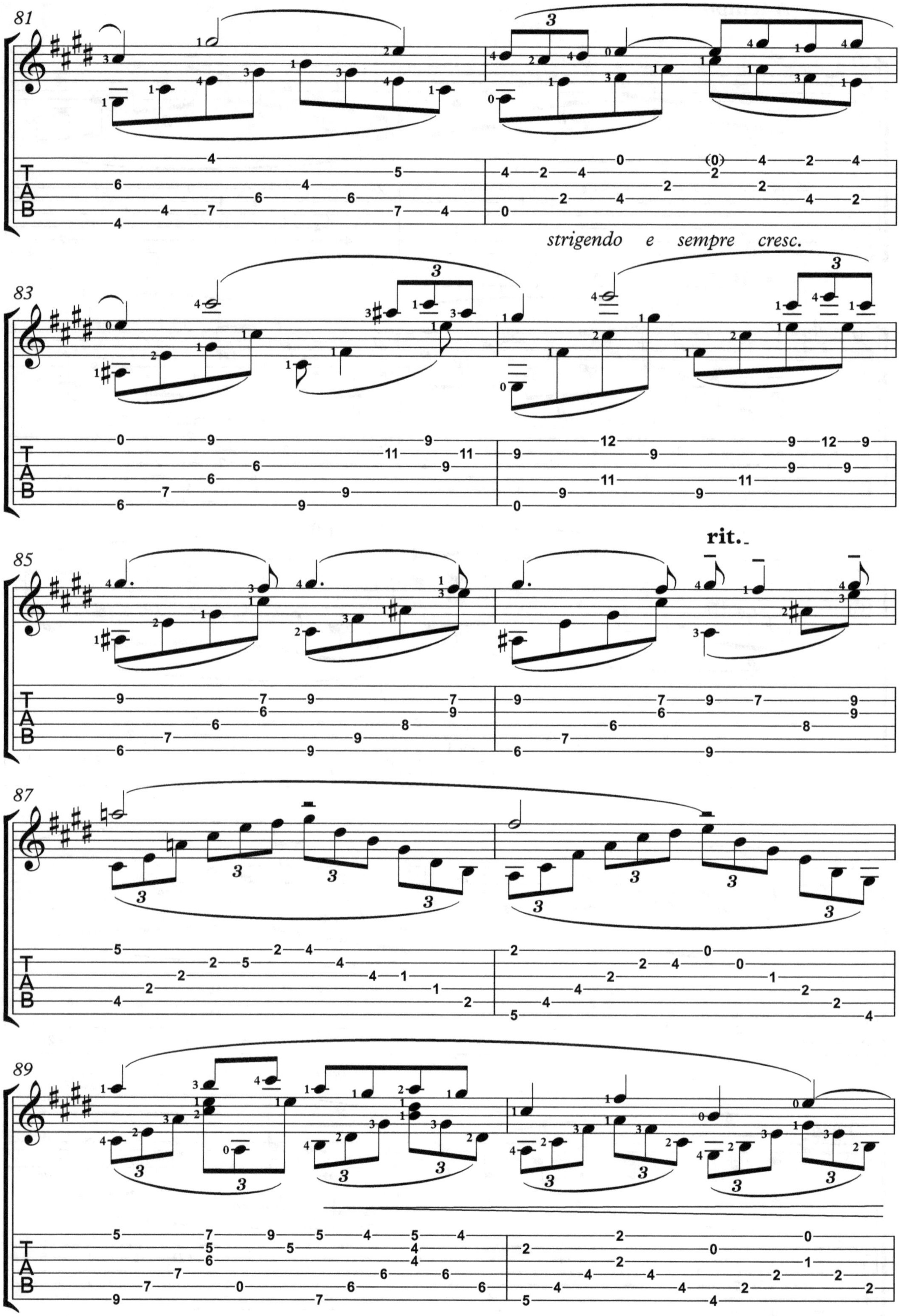
strigendo e sempre cresc.
rit.

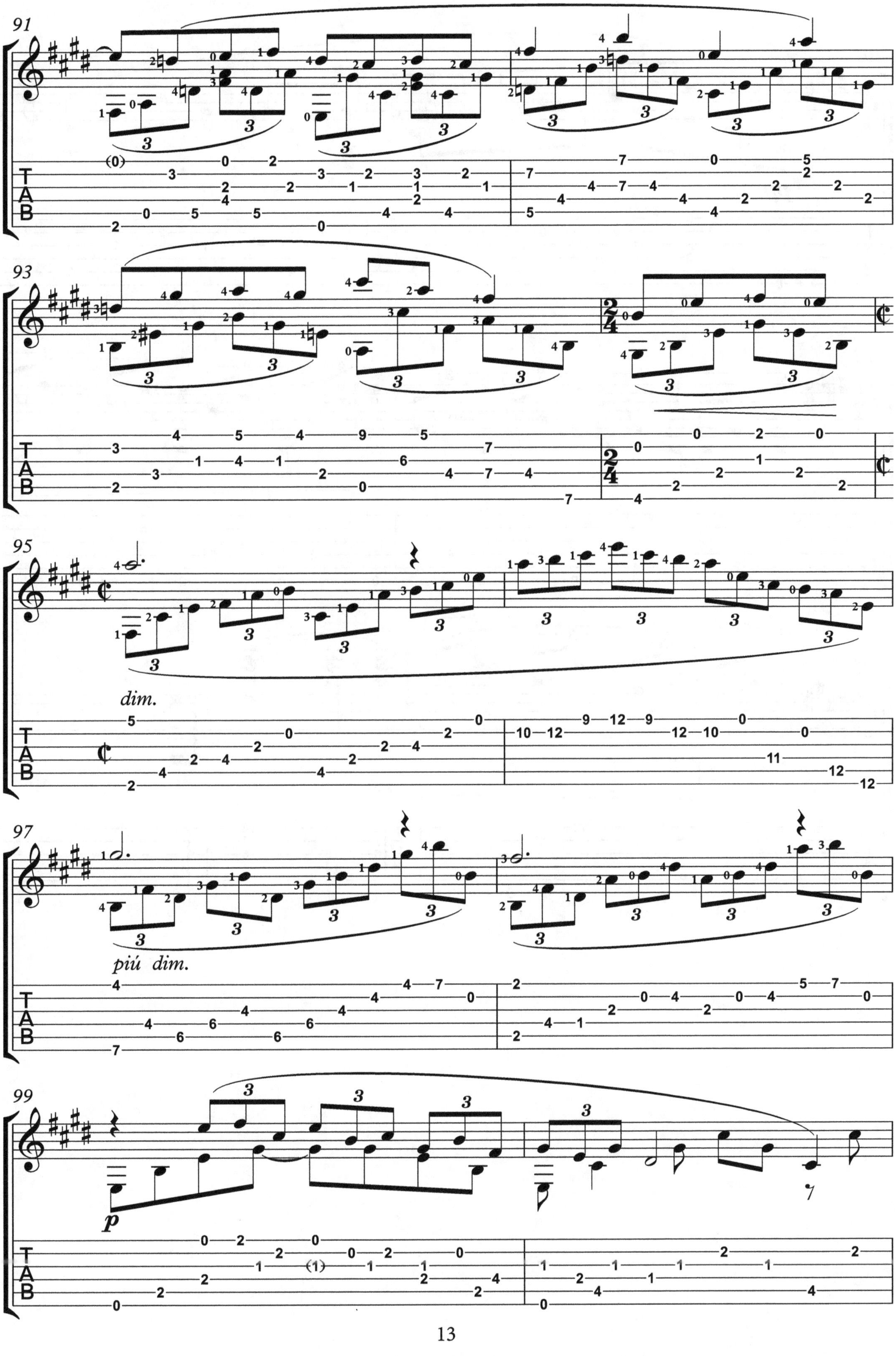
dim.
piú dim.

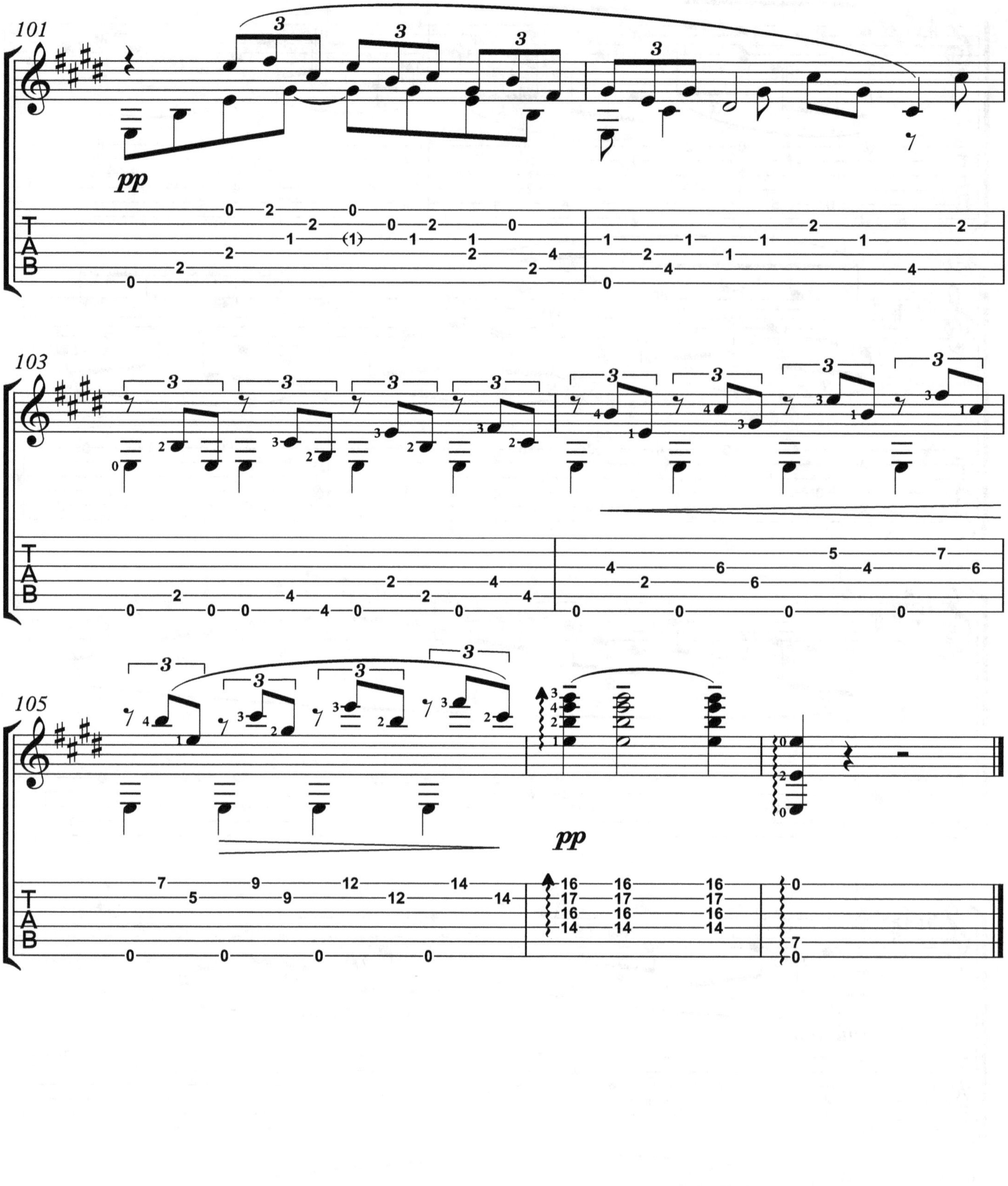
101
pp
TAB
103
105
pp

This page has been left blank to avoid an awkward page turn.

Clair de Lune

Claude Debussy
(1862-1918)

Arranger - Yago Santos

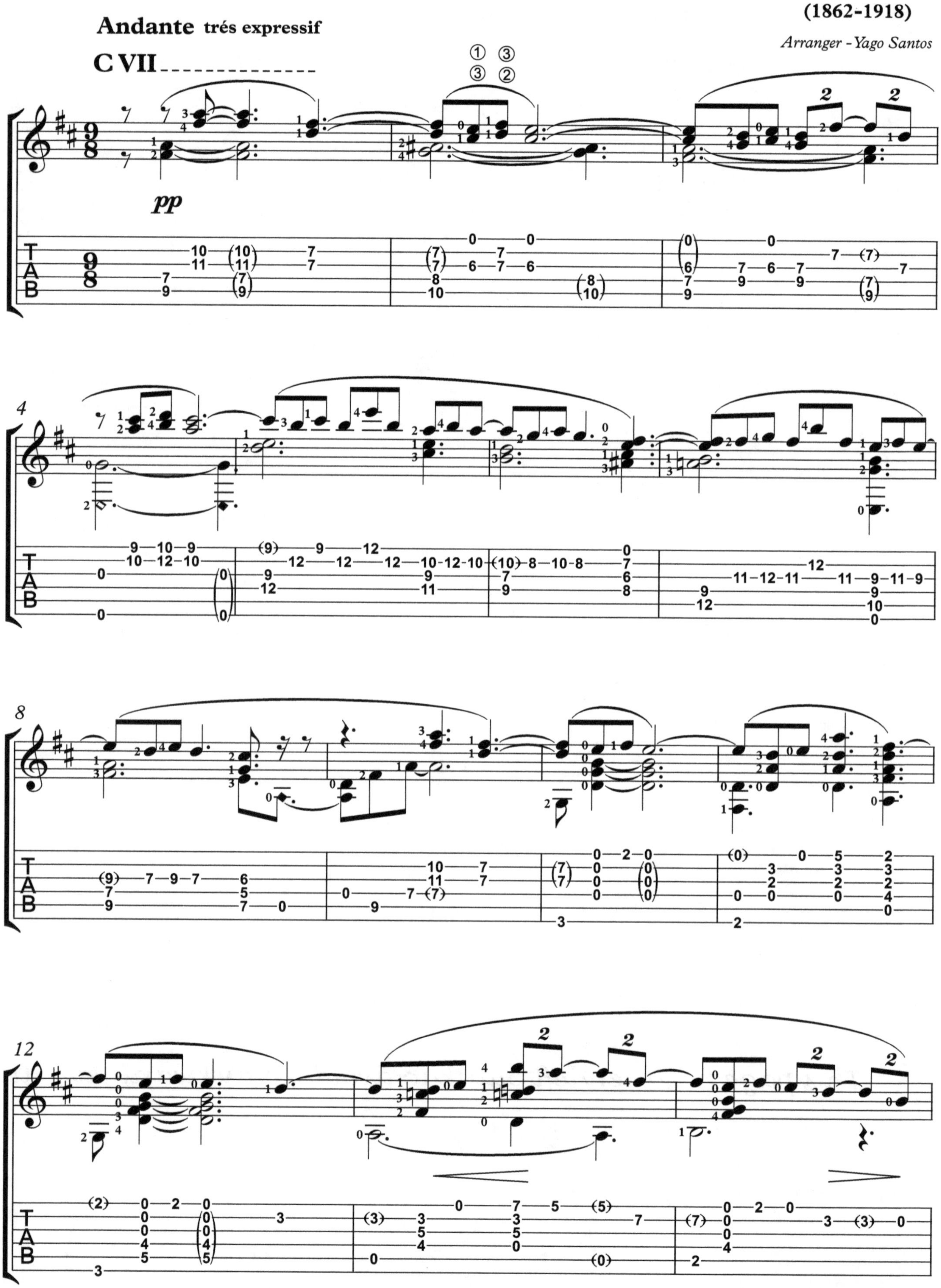

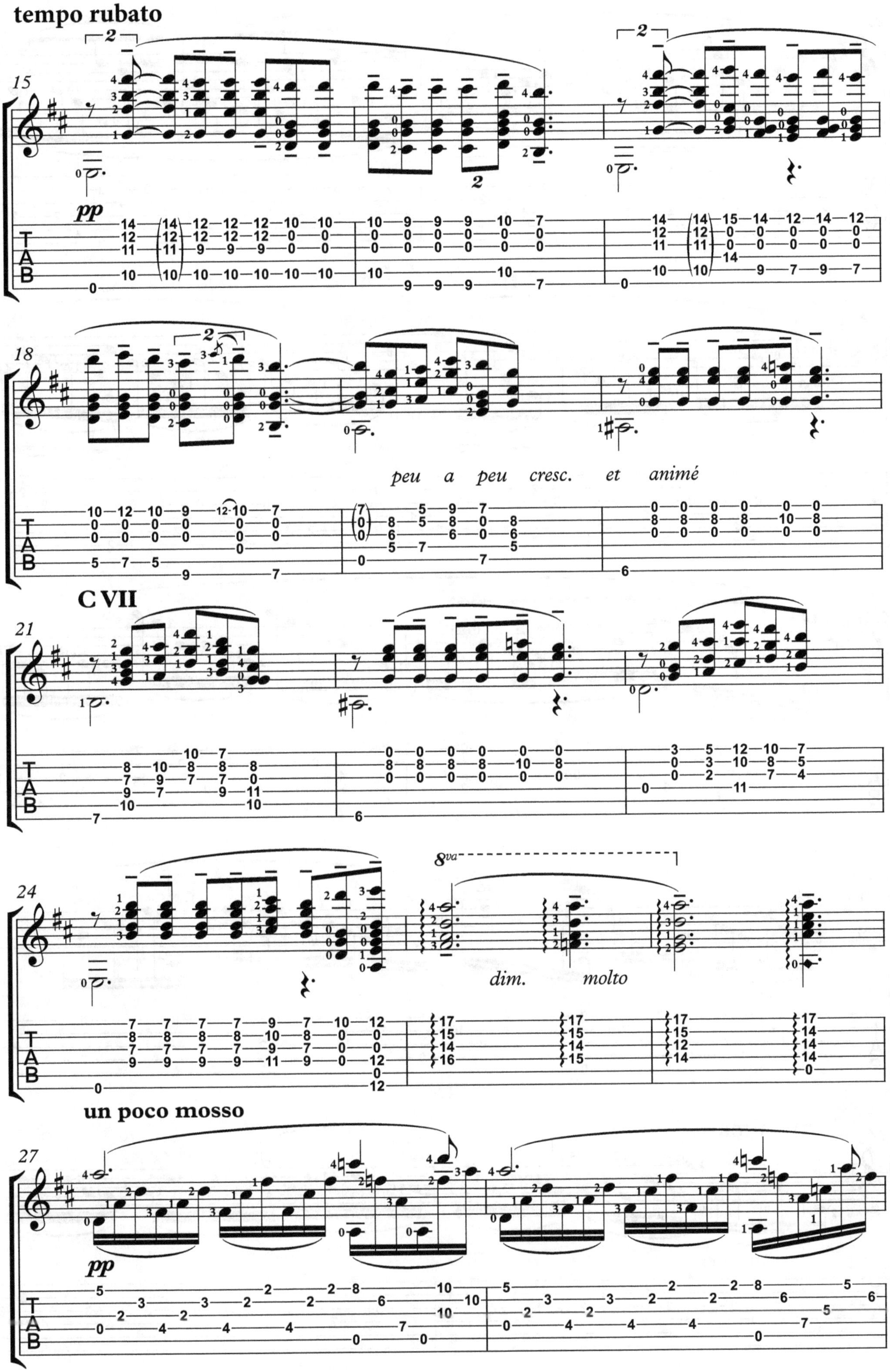
tempo rubato
pp
peu a peu cresc. et animé
C VII
8va
dim. molto
un poco mosso
pp

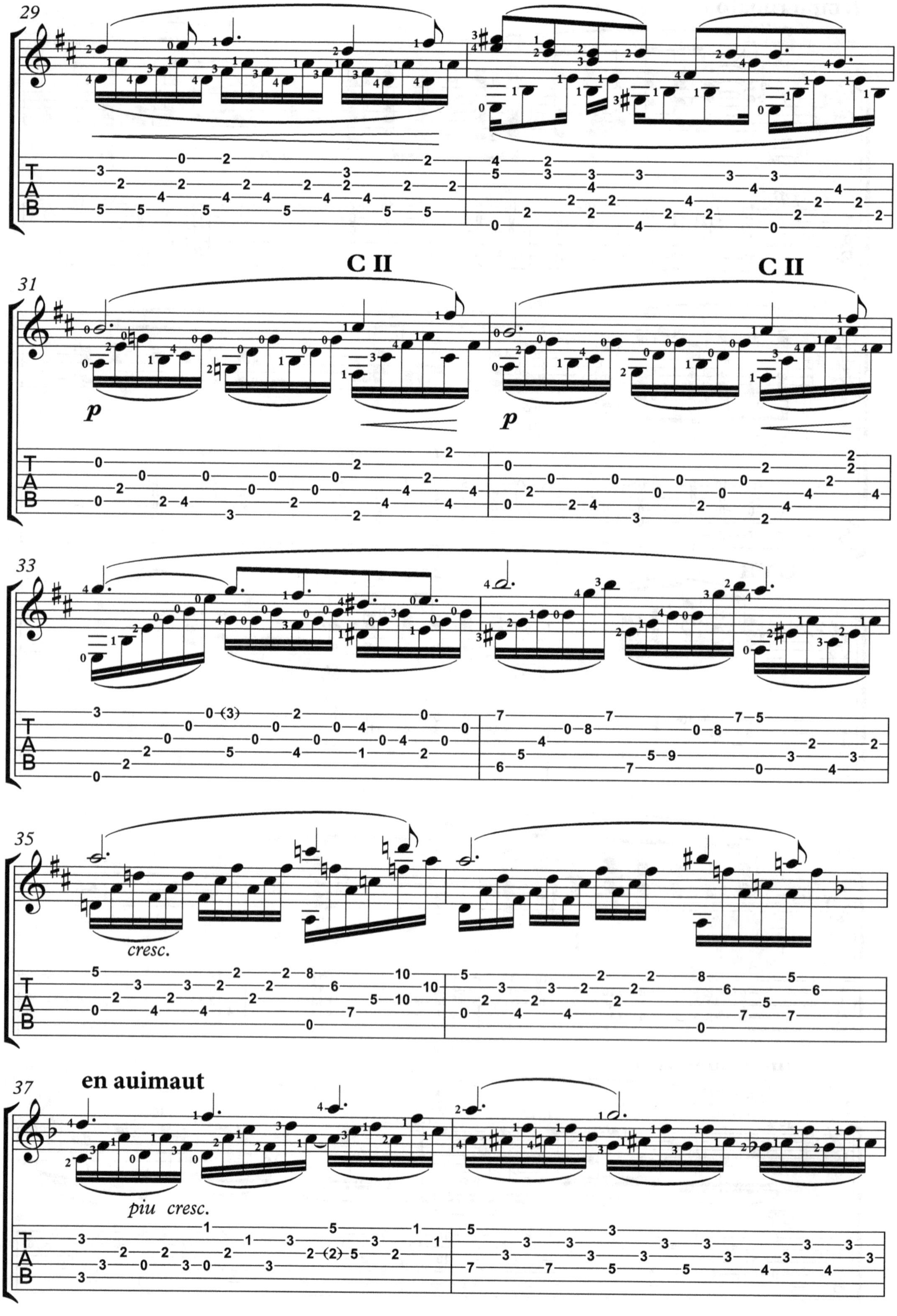
29
31
C II
C II
p
p
33
35
cresc.
37
en auimaut
piu cresc.

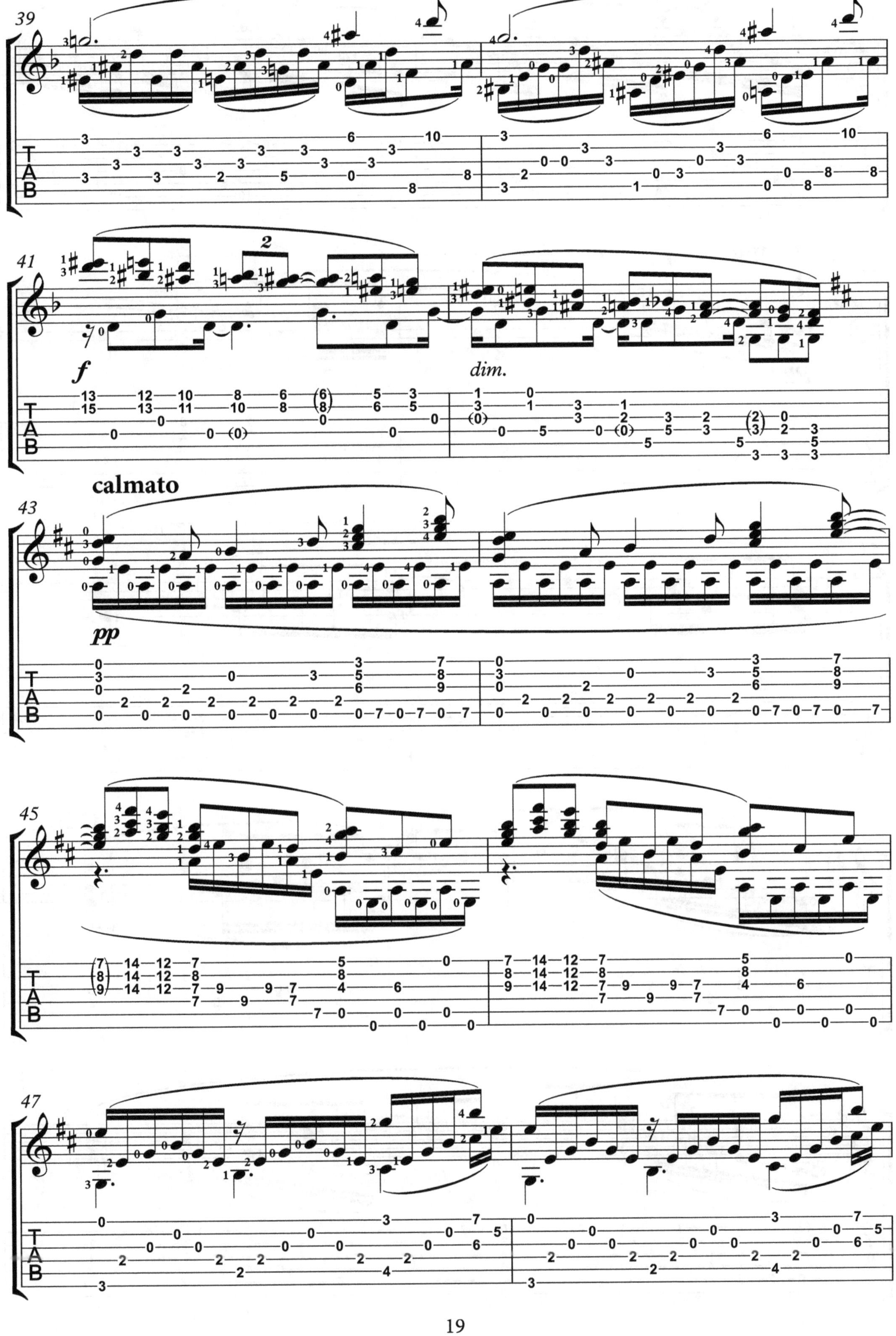
f
dim.
calmato
pp

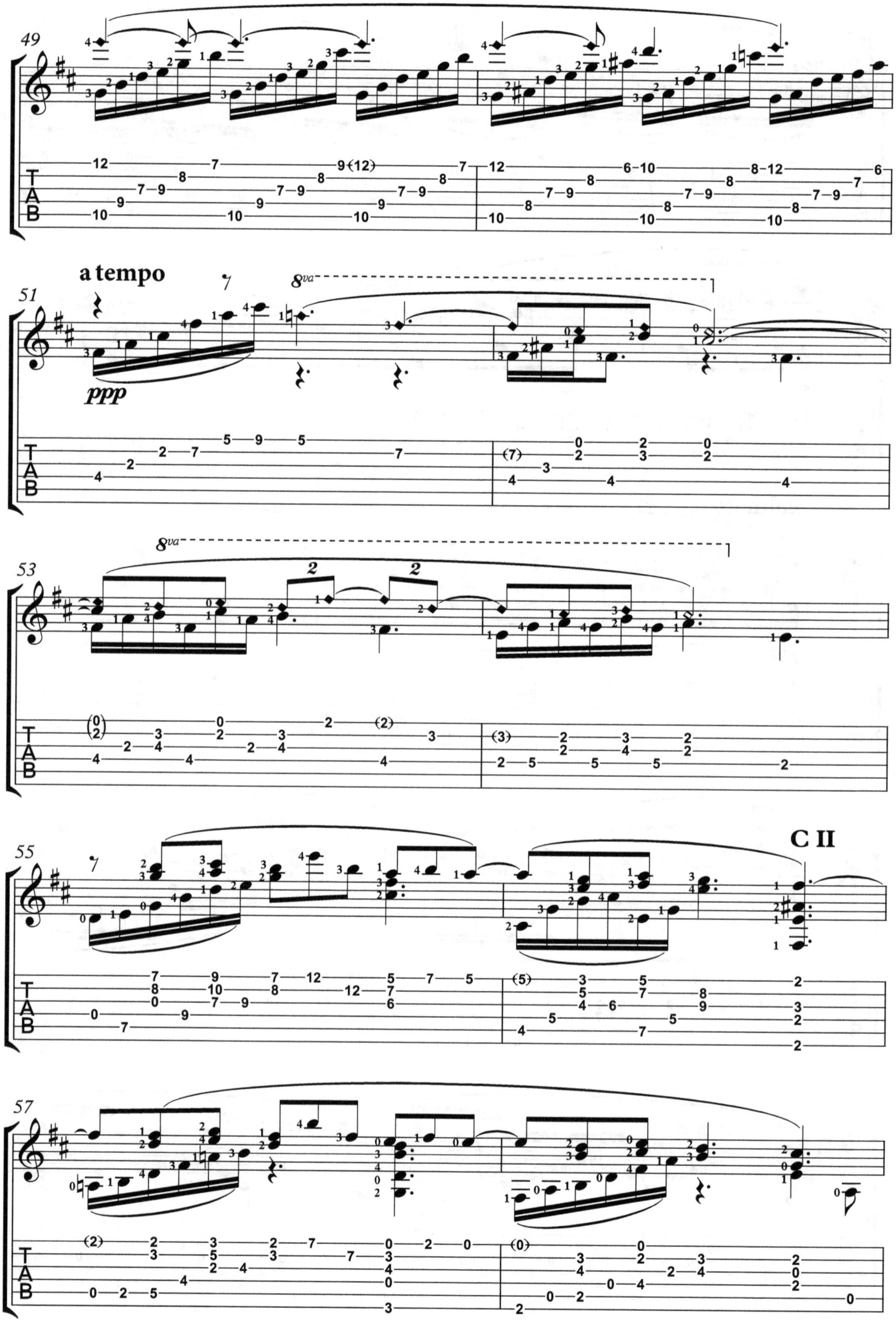
a tempo
ppp
8va
8va
C II

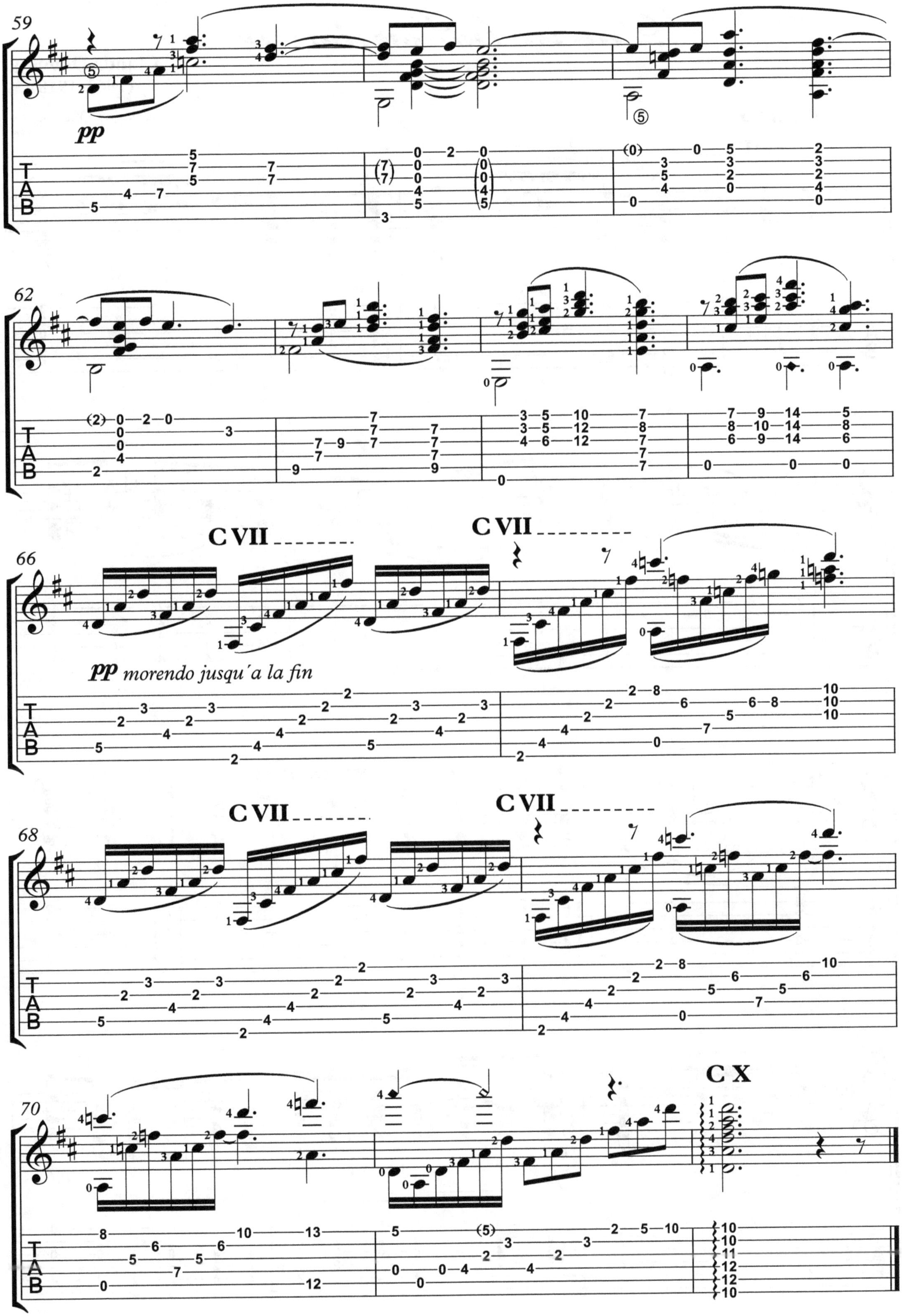
59
pp
62
66
C VII
pp morendo jusqu´a la fin
68
70
C X

Danse bohémienne

Claude Debussy
(1862-1918)

Arranger - Yago Santos

Allegro

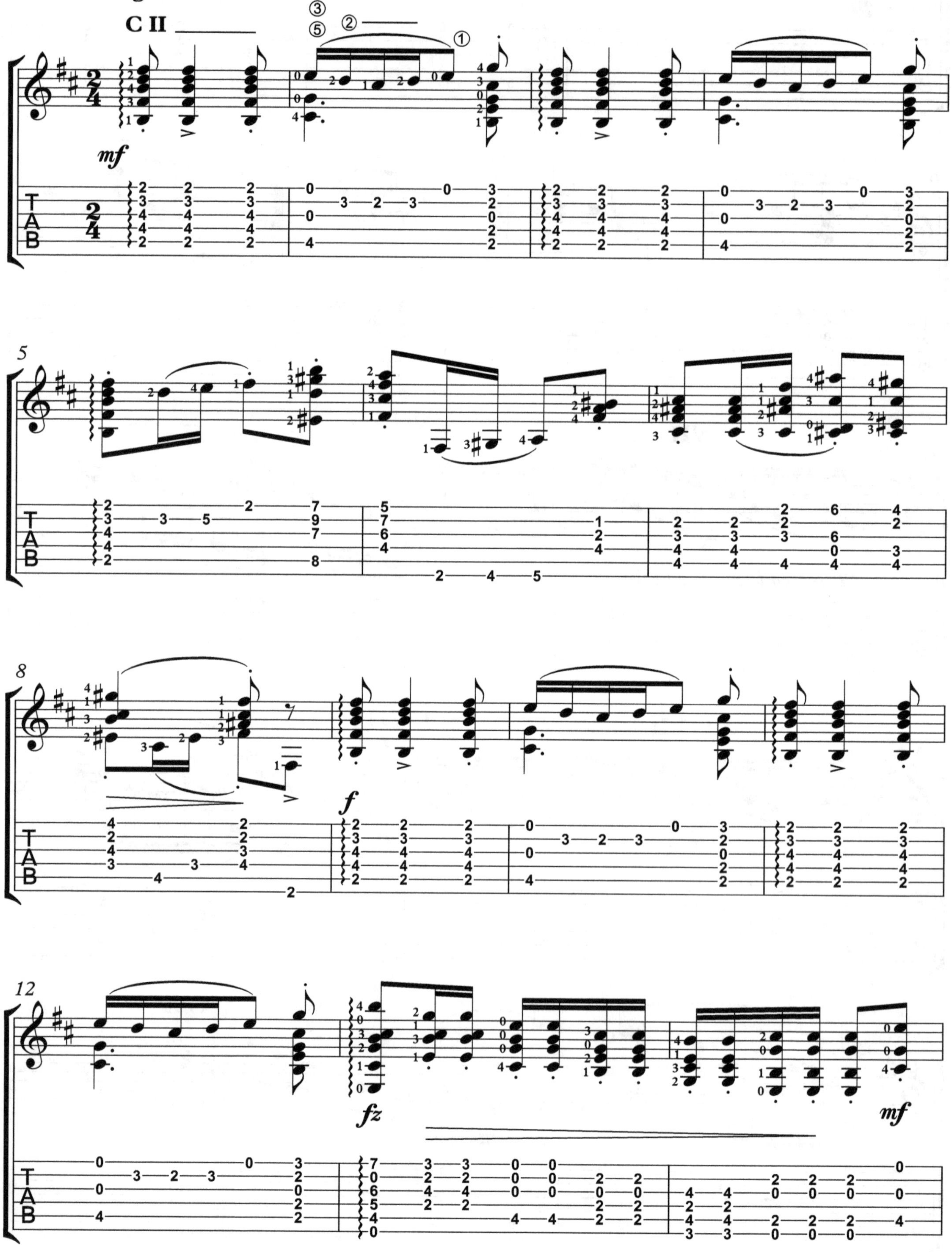

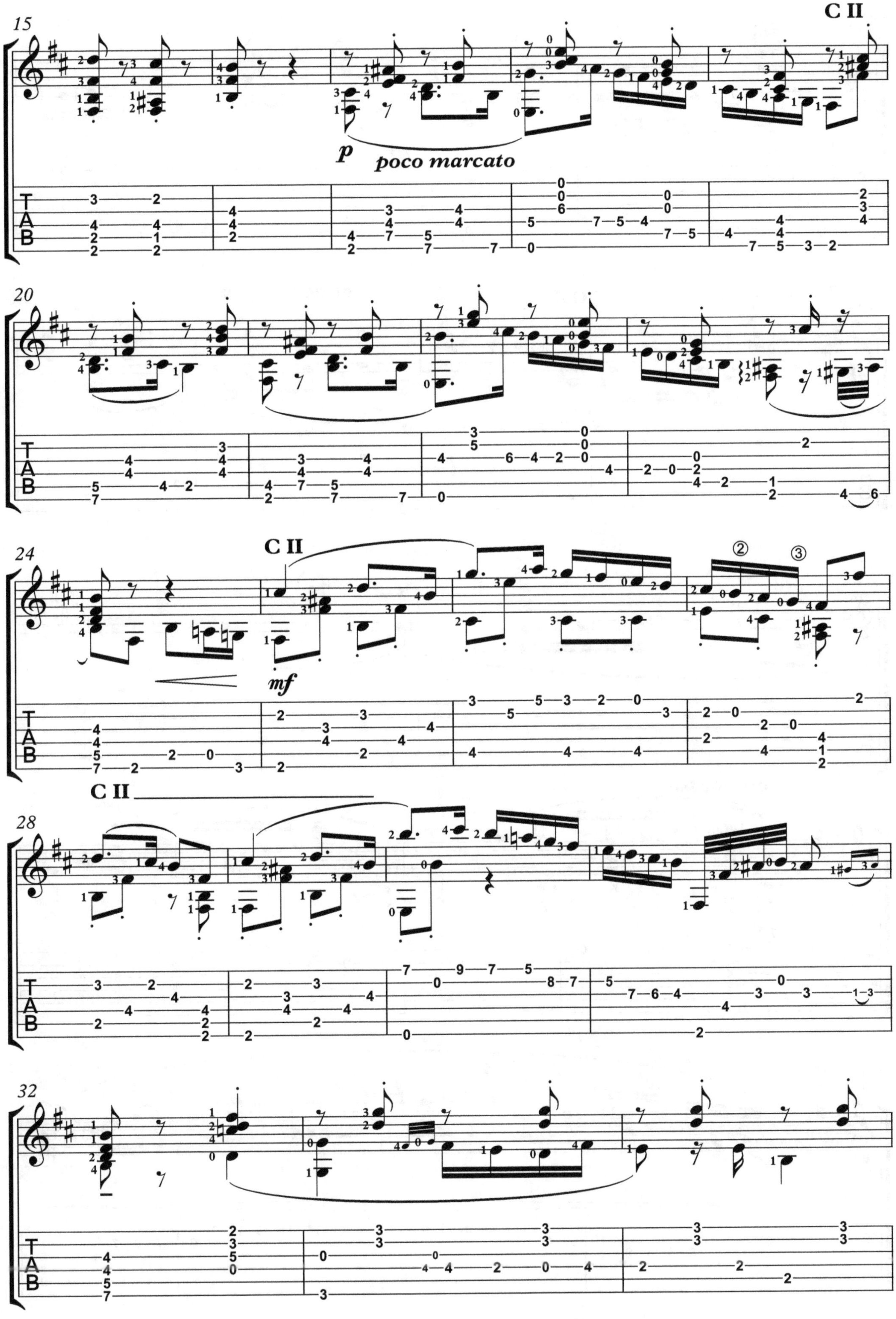
C II
poco marcato
C II
C II

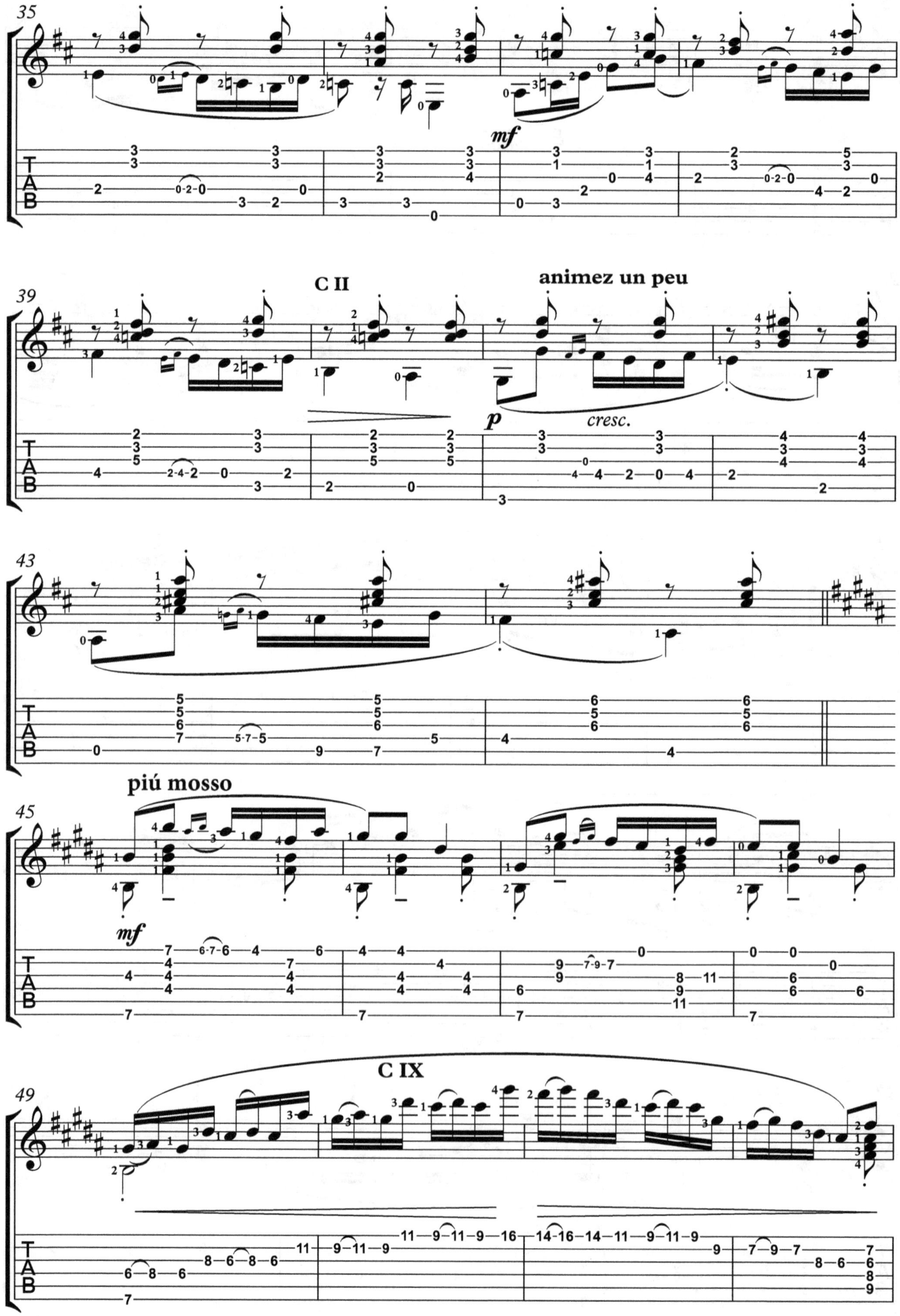
35
mf
39
C II
animez un peu
p
cresc.
43
piú mosso
45
mf
49
C IX

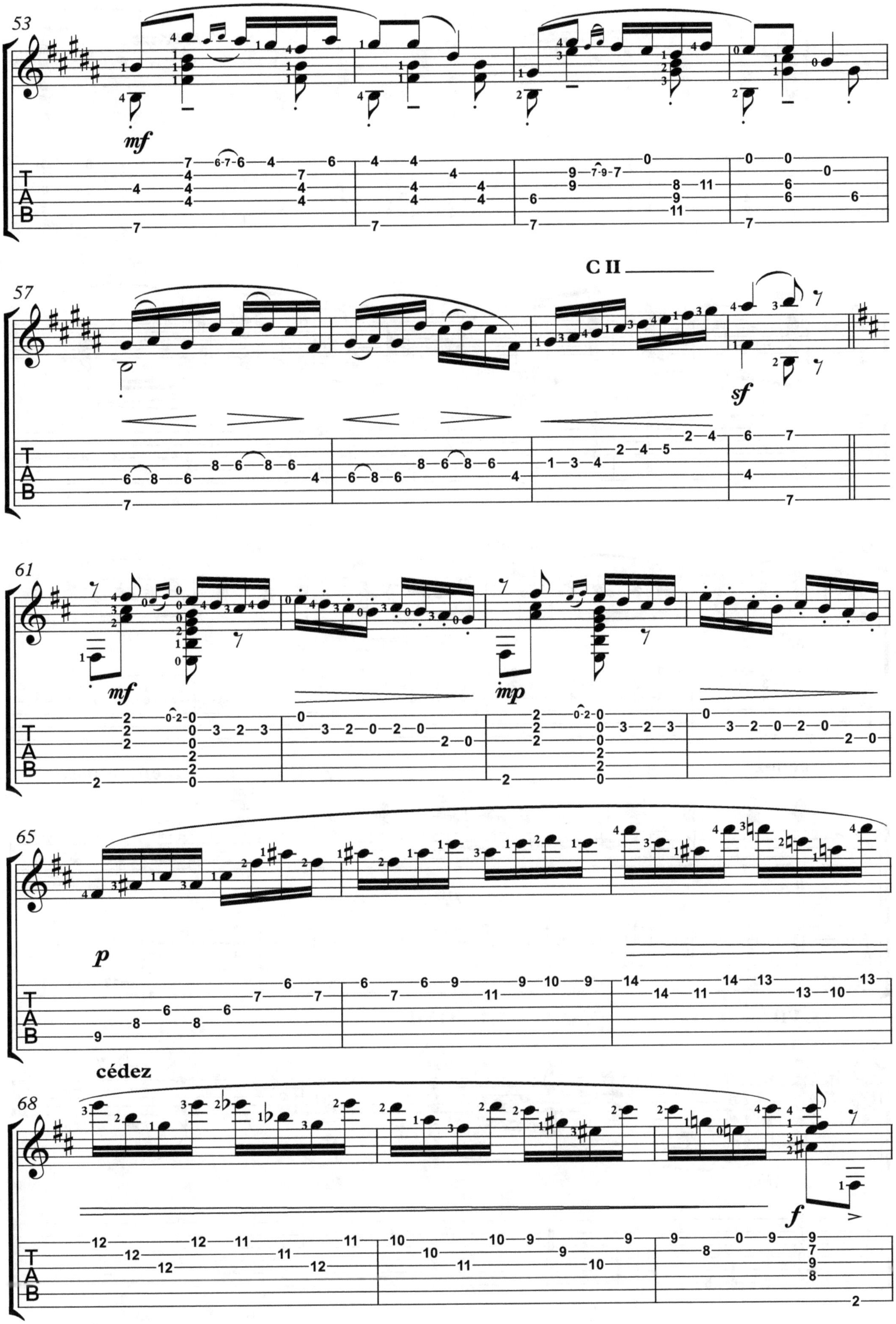
53
mf
57
C II
sf
61
mf
mp
65
p
cédez
68
f

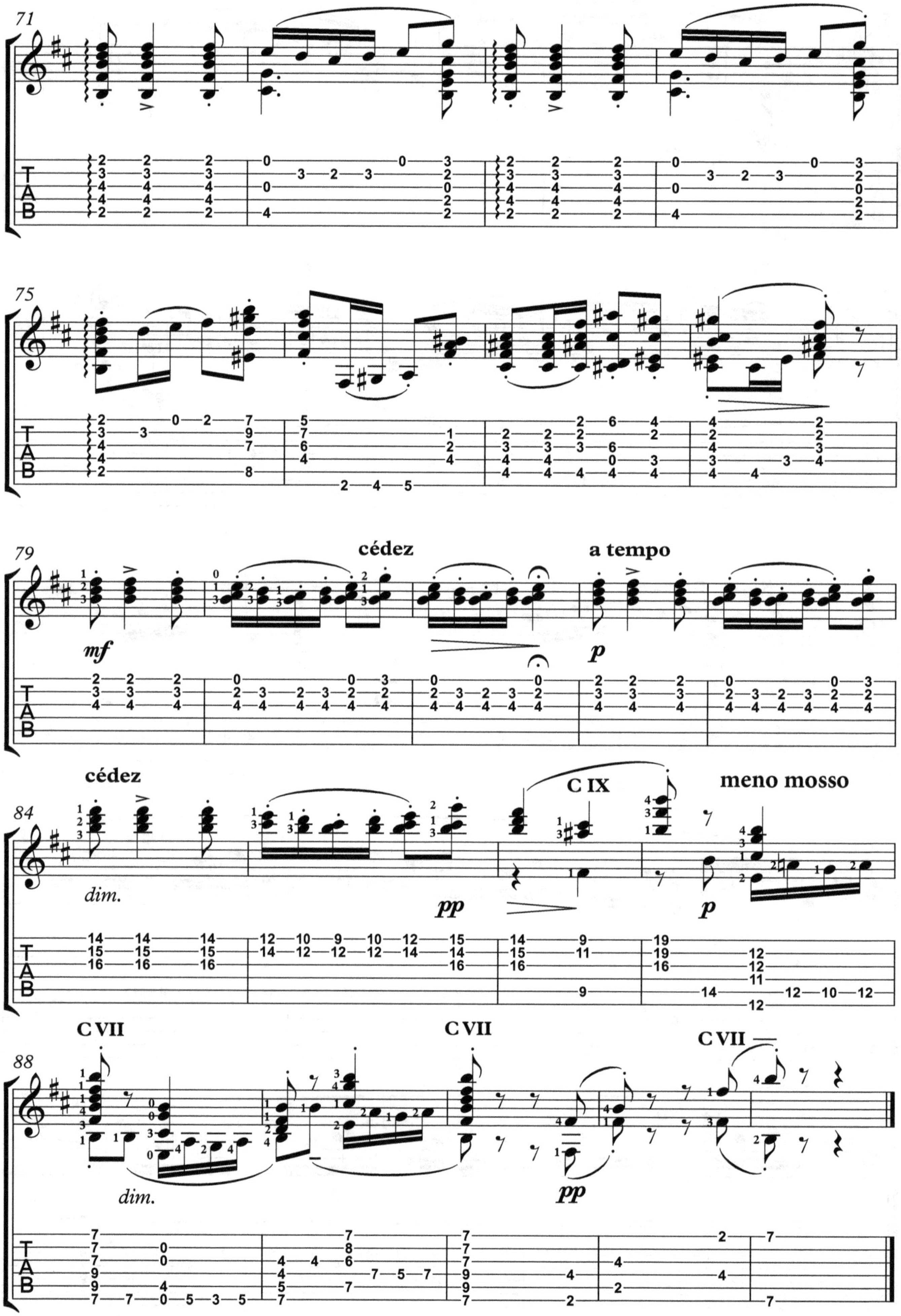
cédez
a tempo
mf
p
cédez
dim.
pp
C IX
meno mosso
p
C VII
C VII
C VII —
dim.
pp

This page has been left blank to avoid an awkward page turn.

Children's Corner

Doctor Gradus ad Parnassum

(1908)

Claude Debussy
(1862-1918)

Arranger - Yago Santos

⑥ → C

Modérement animé Presto

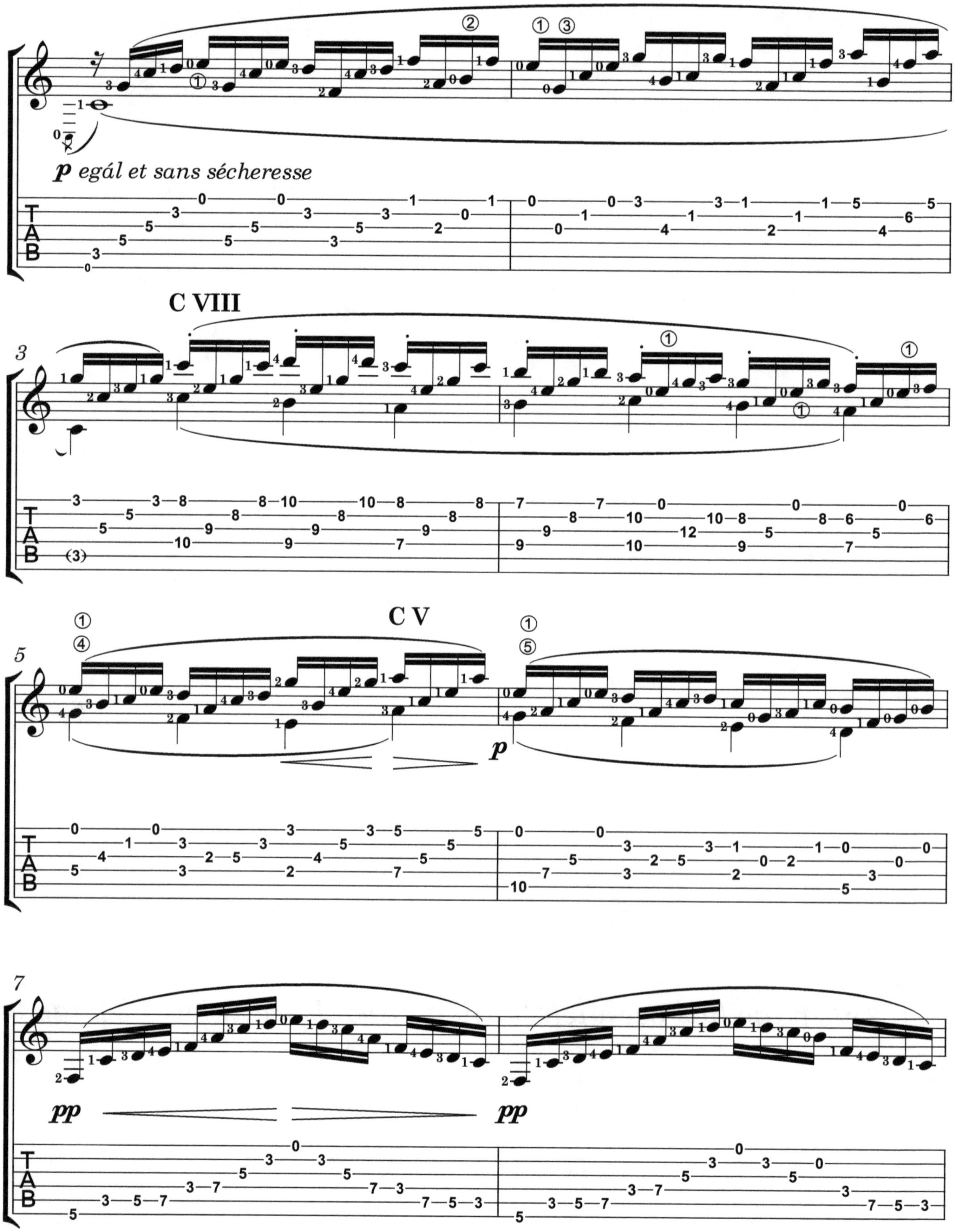

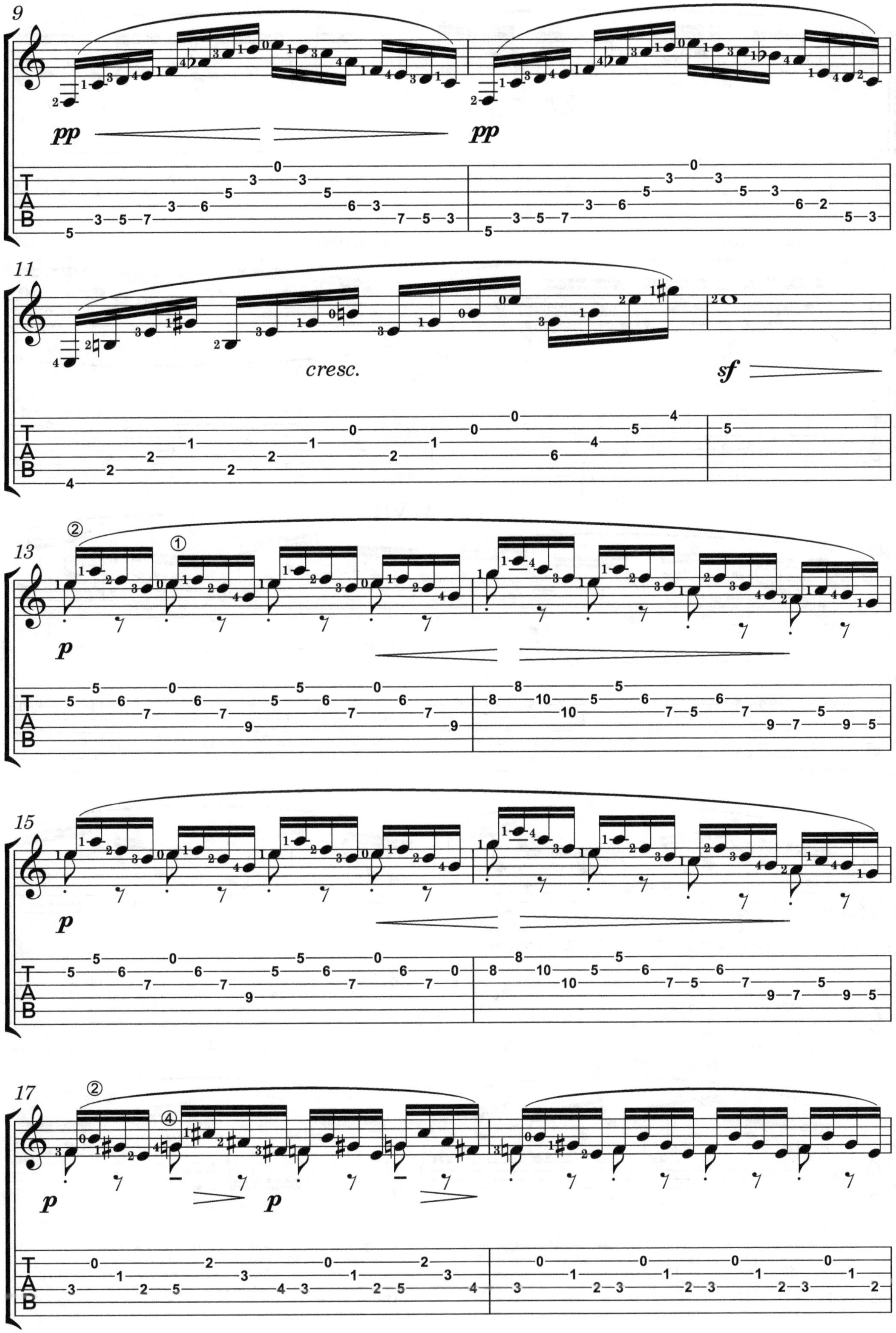
9
pp
pp
11
cresc.
sf
13
p
15
p
17
p
p

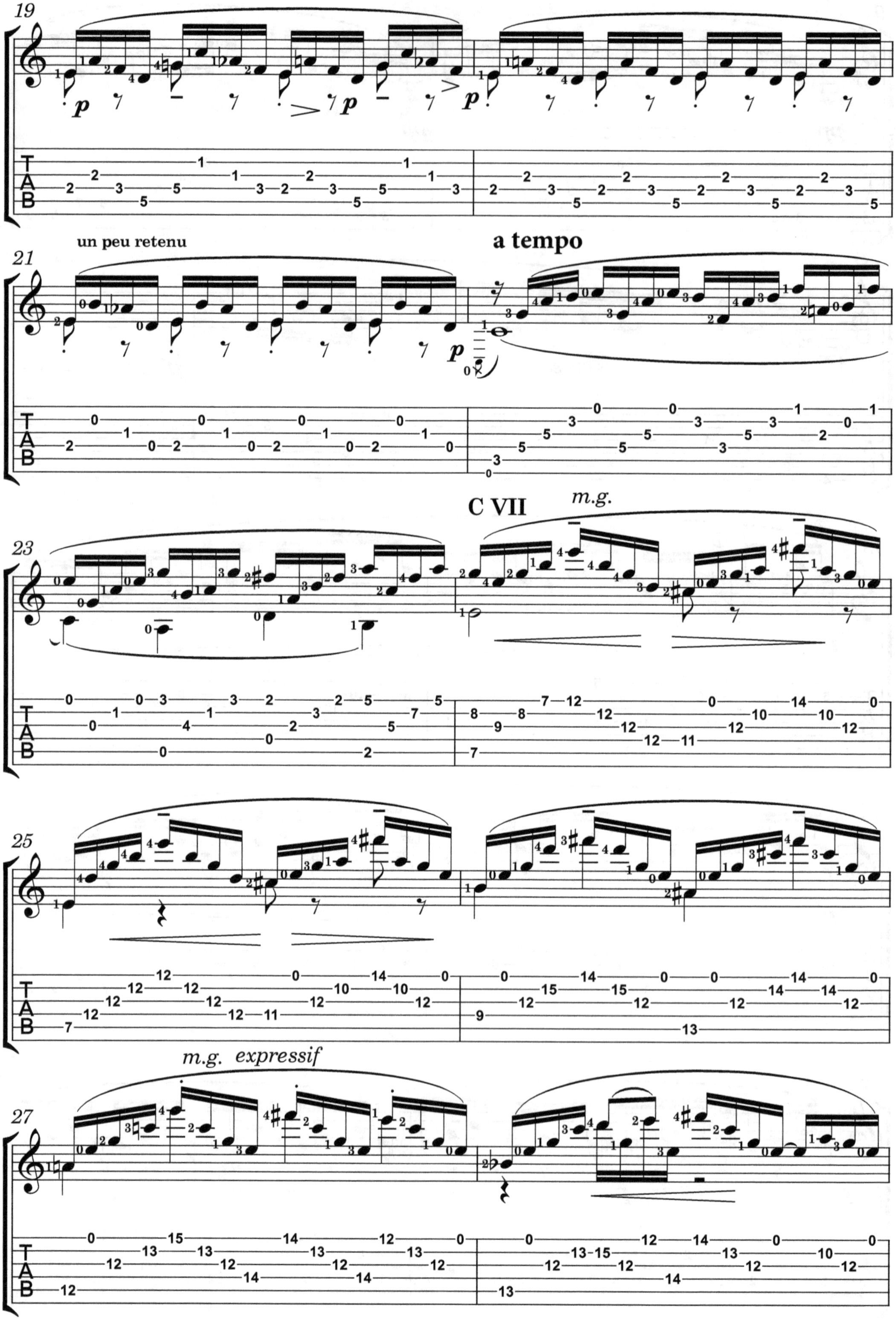
un peu retenu
a tempo
C VII
m.g.
m.g. expressif

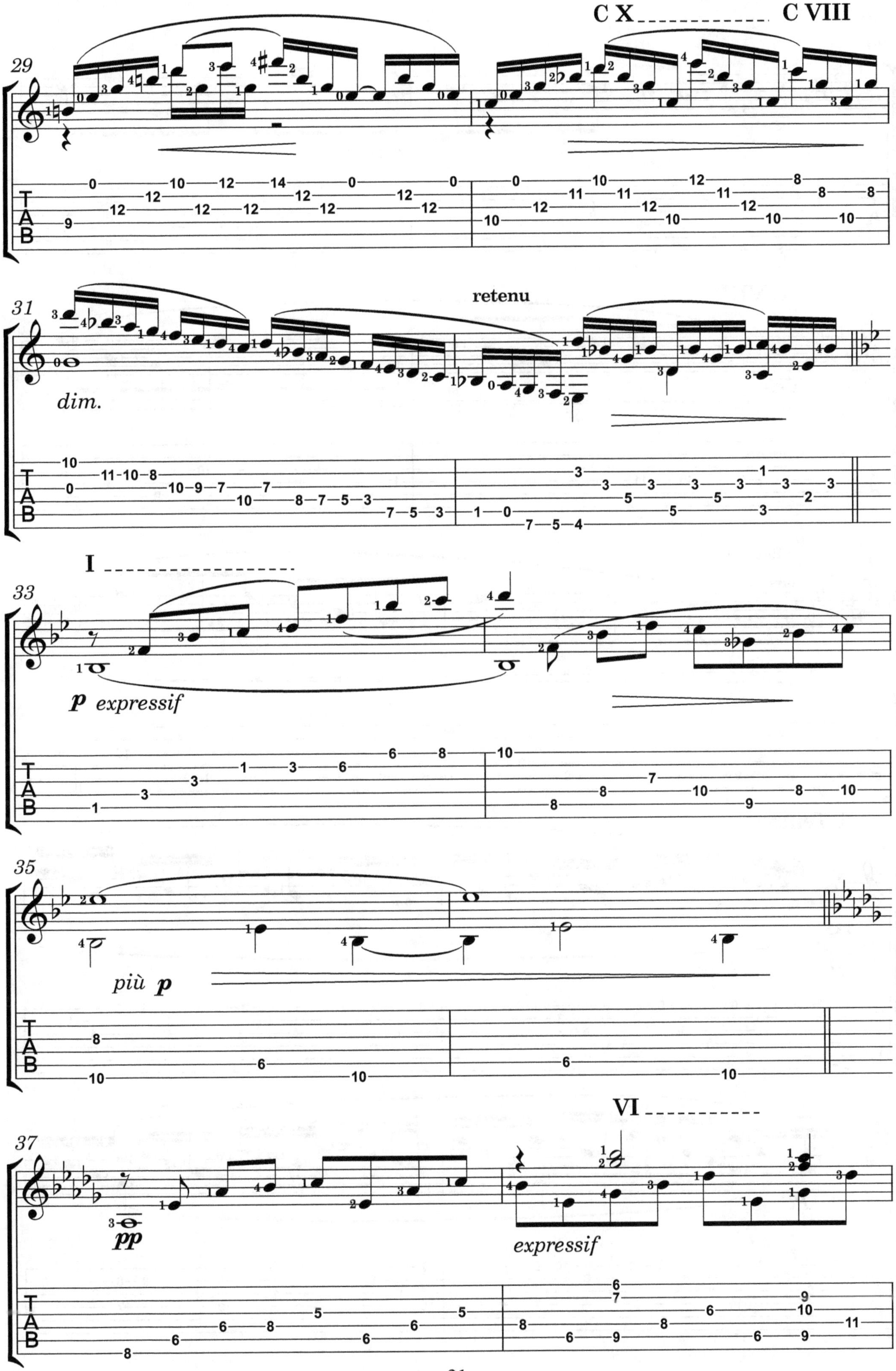
C X
C VIII
retenu
dim.
I
p expressif
più p
VI
pp
expressif

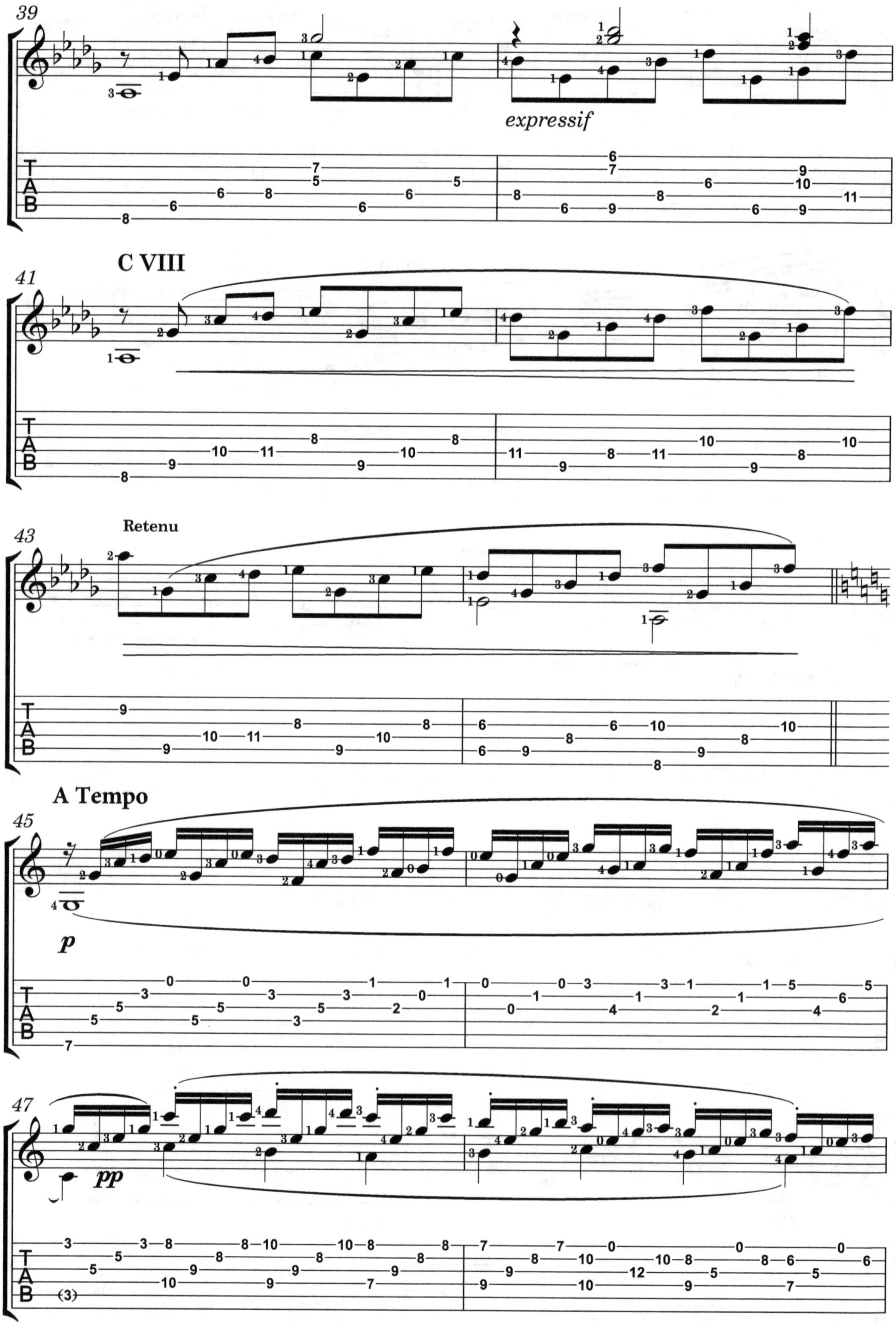
39
expressif
41
C VIII
43
Retenu
A Tempo
45
p
47
pp

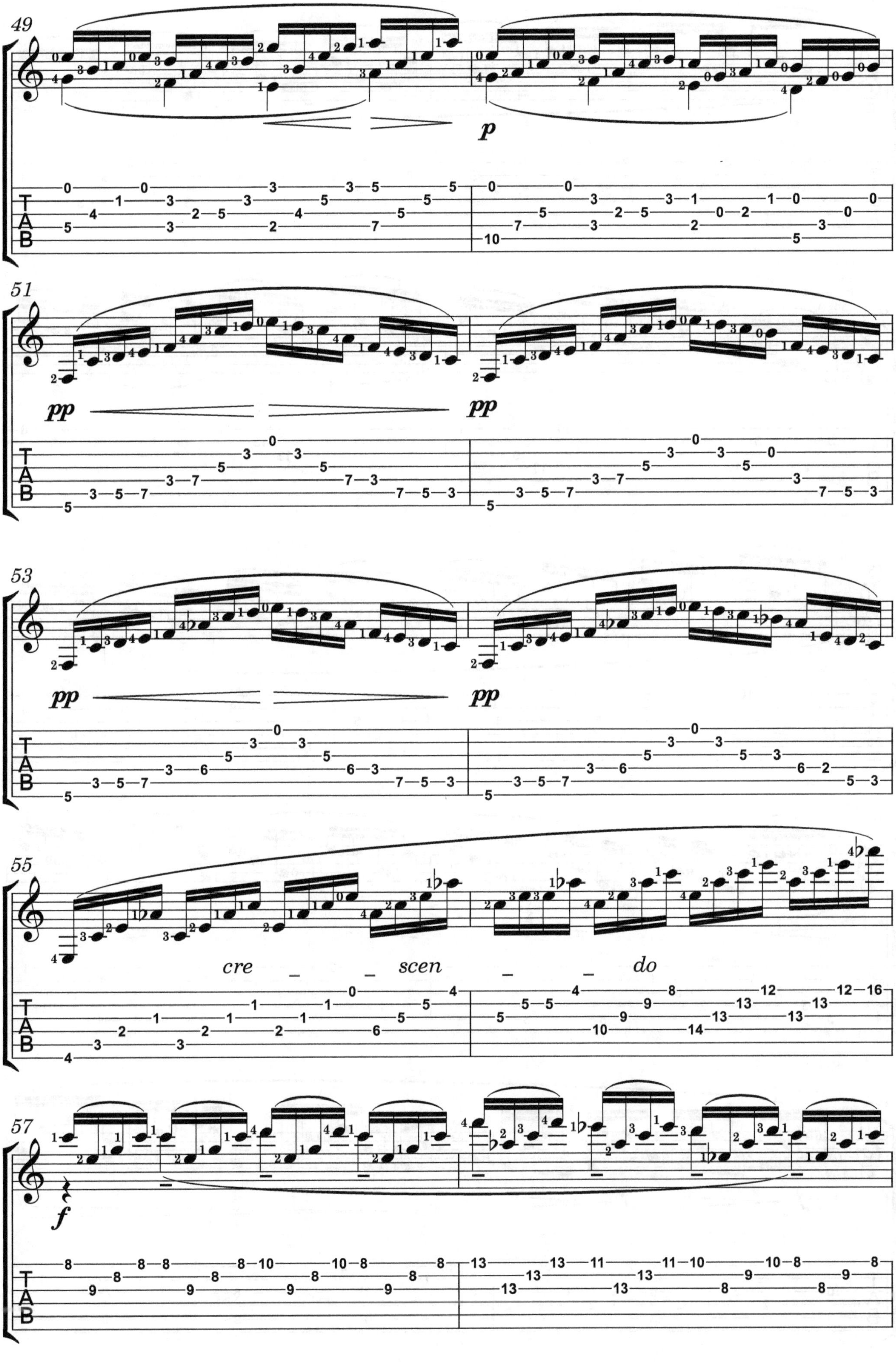
cre _ _ scen _ _ do

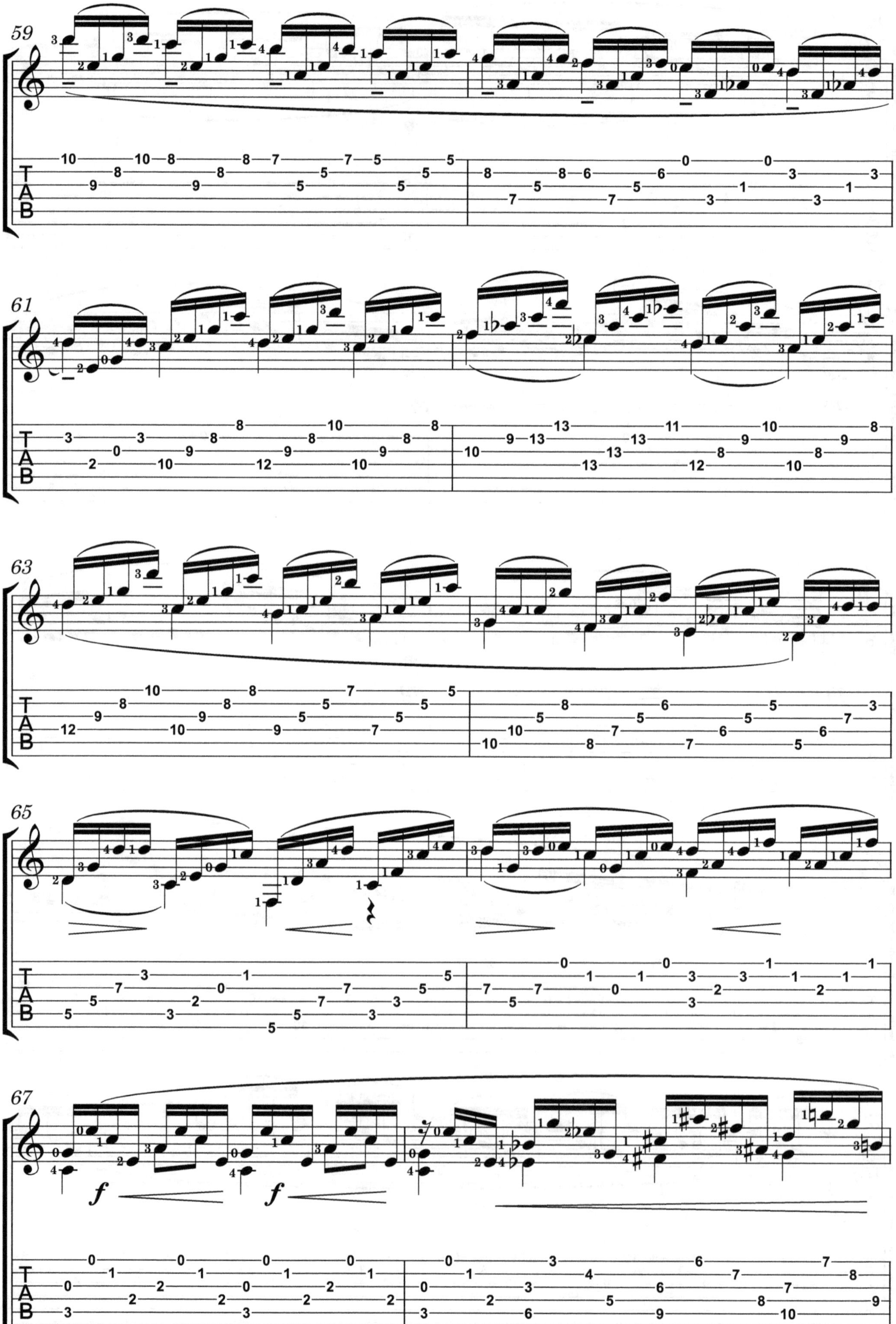
59
61
63
65
67

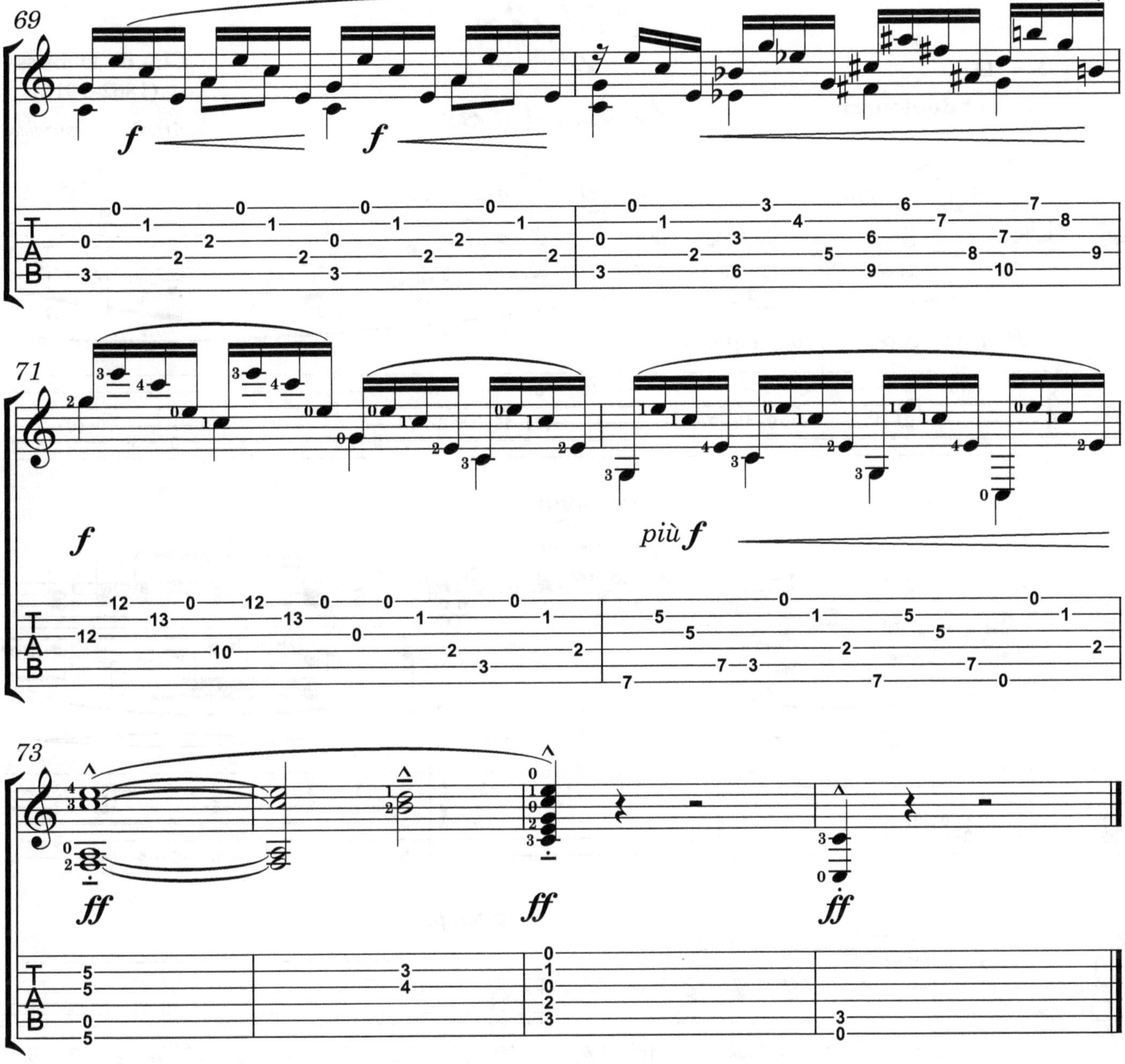
69
71
73
f
più f
ff

Elégie

Lesure No. 138

Claude Debussy
(1862-1918)

Arranger - Yago Santos

⑥ — D

Lent et doulourenx

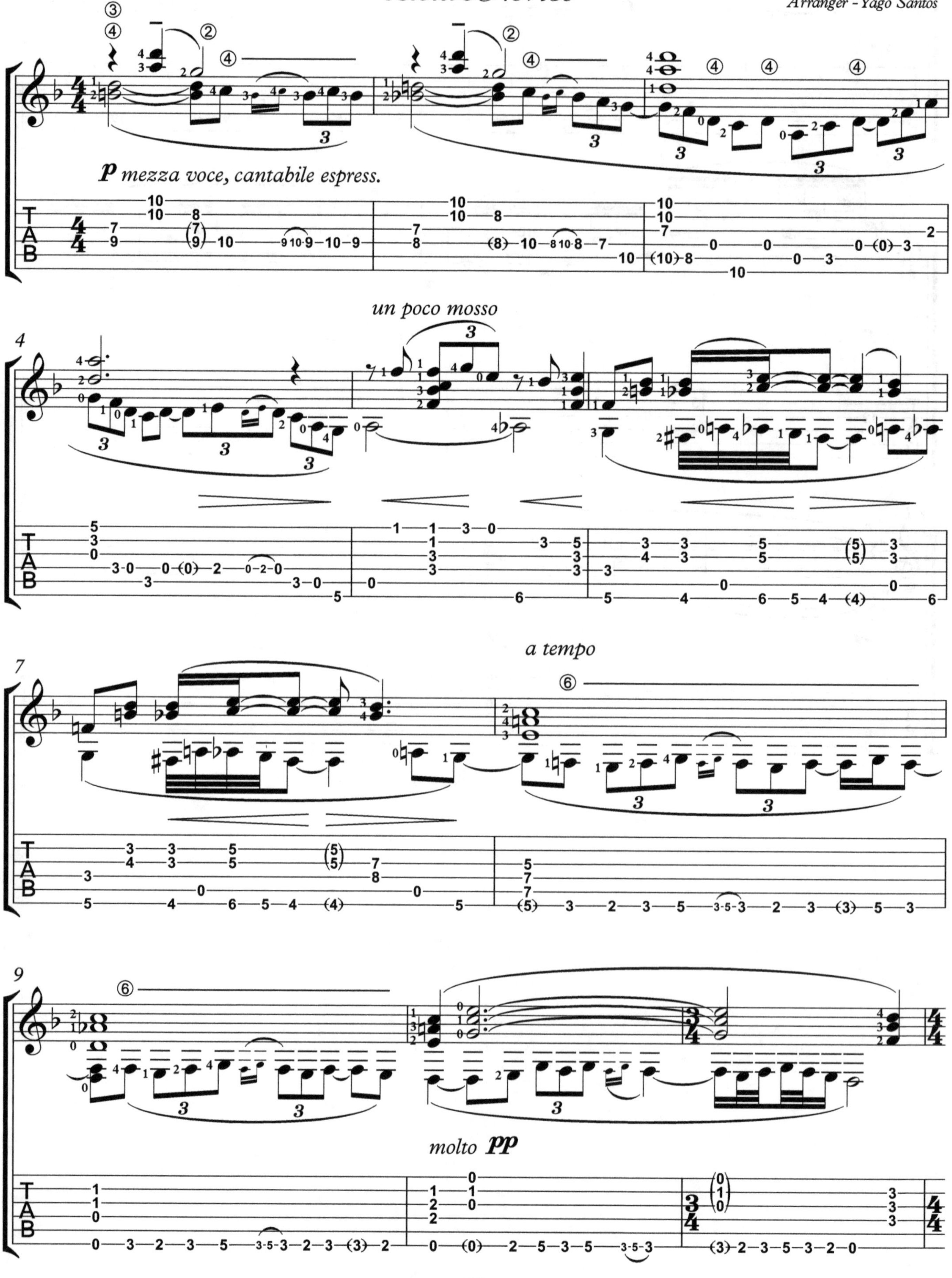

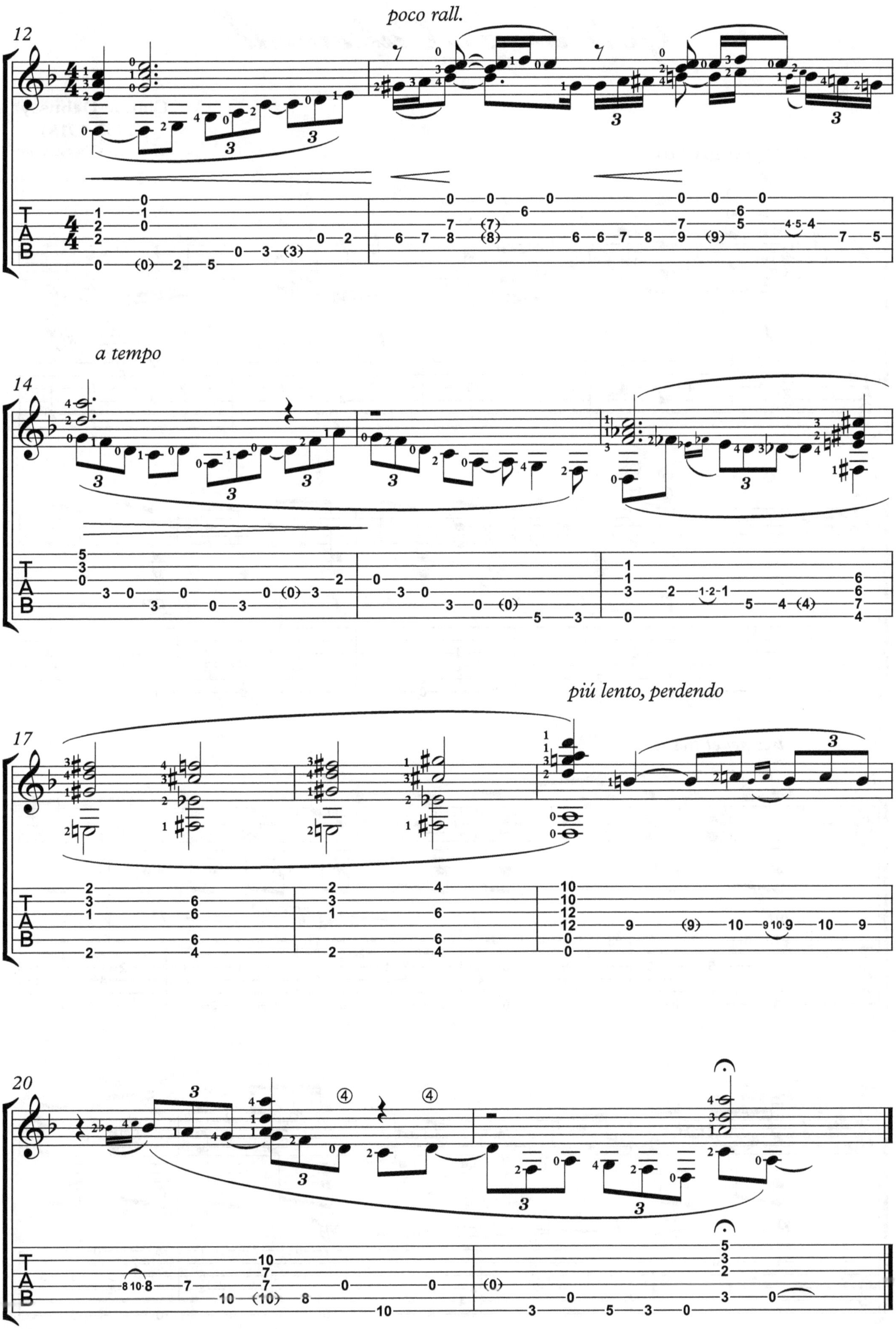
poco rall.
a tempo
piú lento, perdendo

Golliwog's Cakewalk

Claude Debussy
(1862-1918)
Arranger - Yago Santos

Allegro giusto

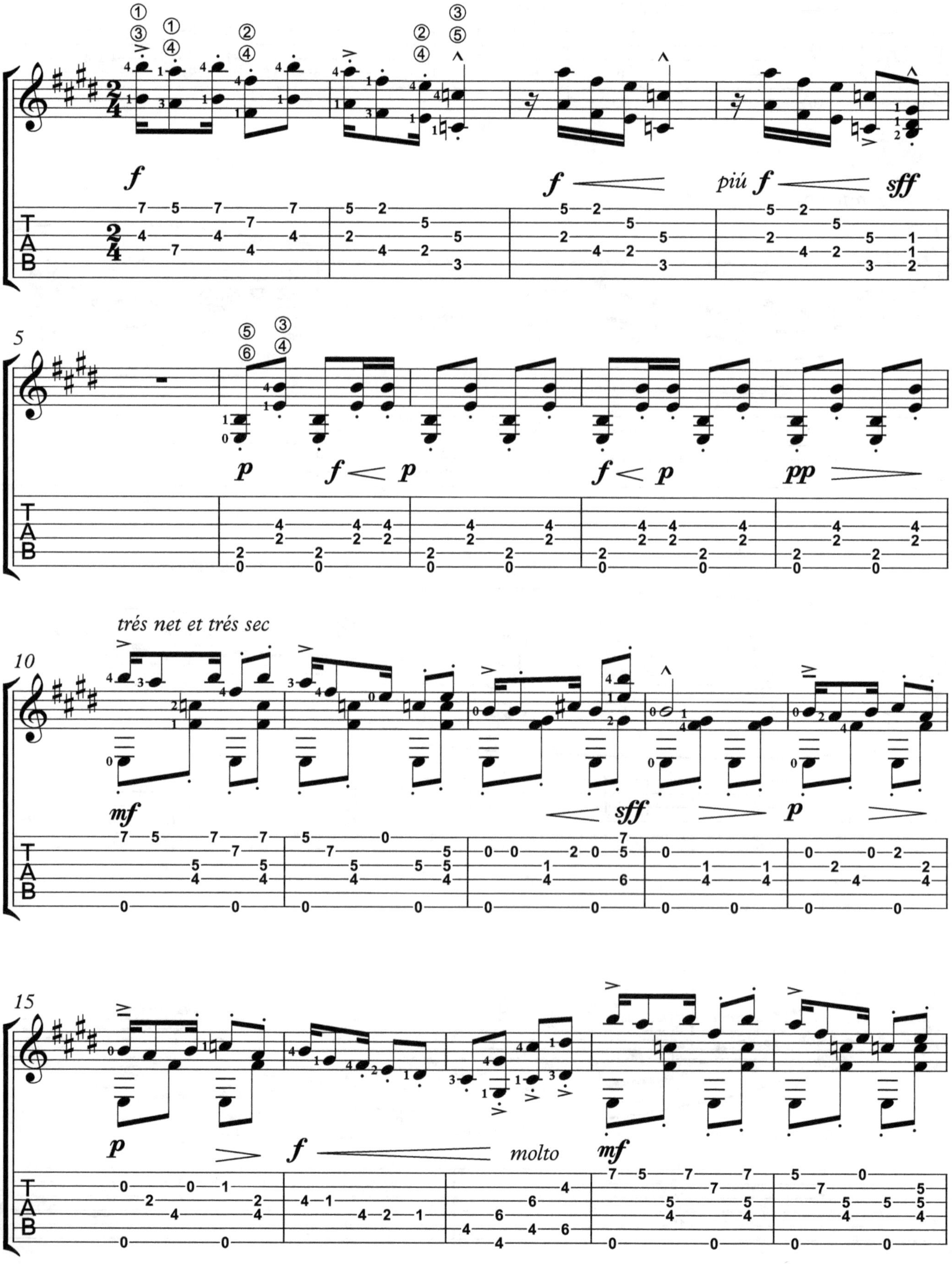

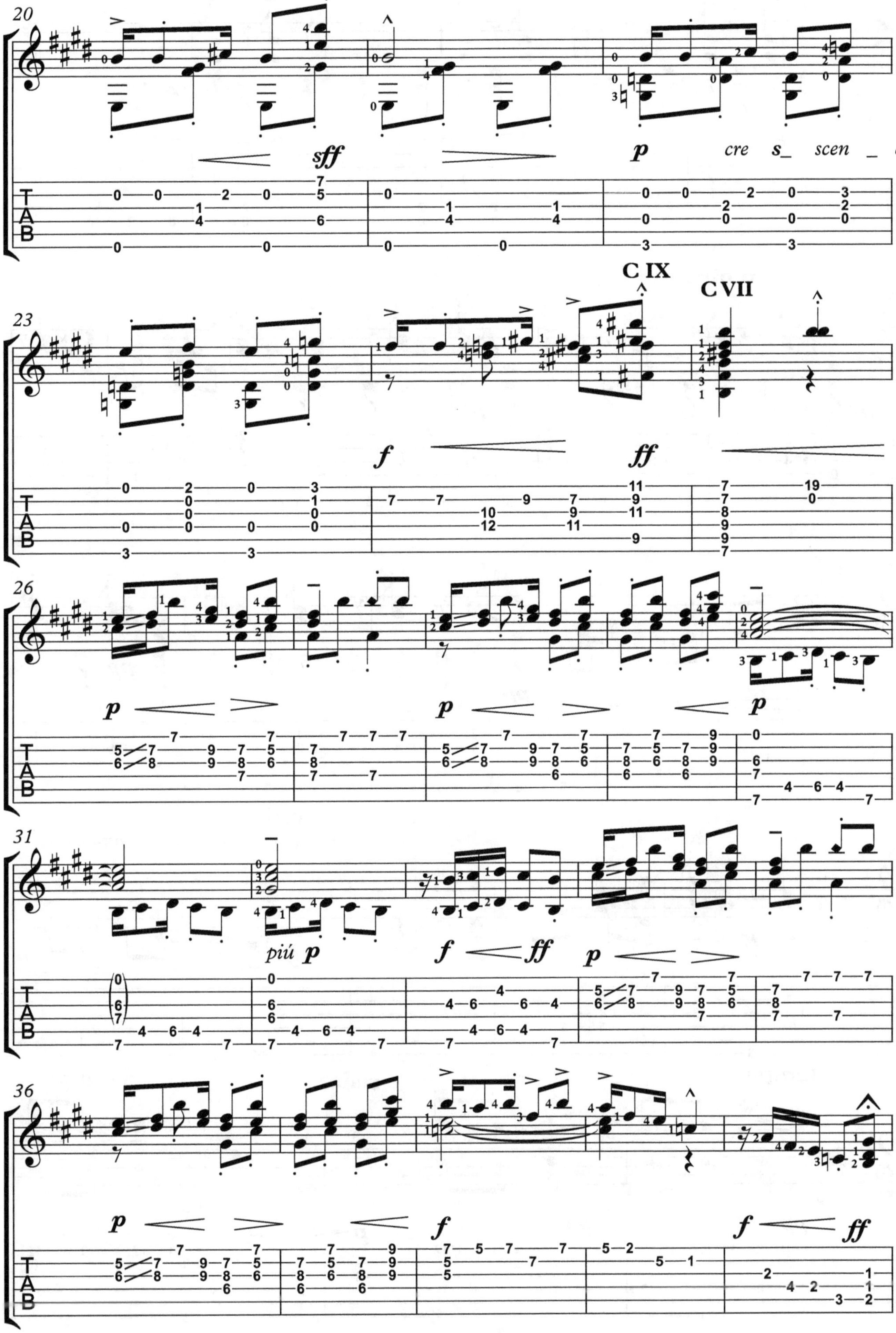
sff
p cre s_ scen _ do
C IX
C VII
f
ff
p
p
piú p
f ff
p
p
f
f ff

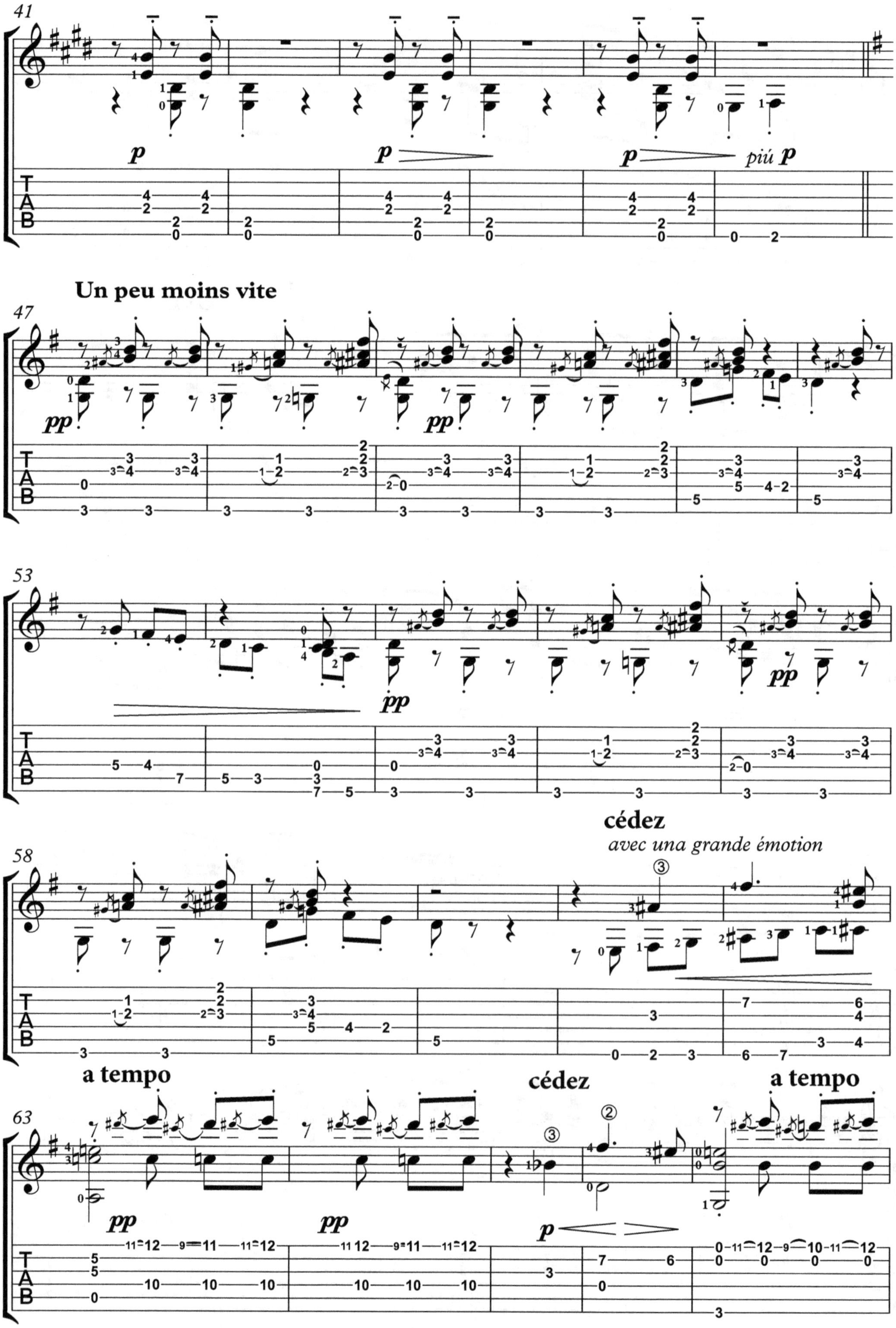
Un peu moins vite
cédez
avec una grande émotion
a tempo
cédez
a tempo
piú p

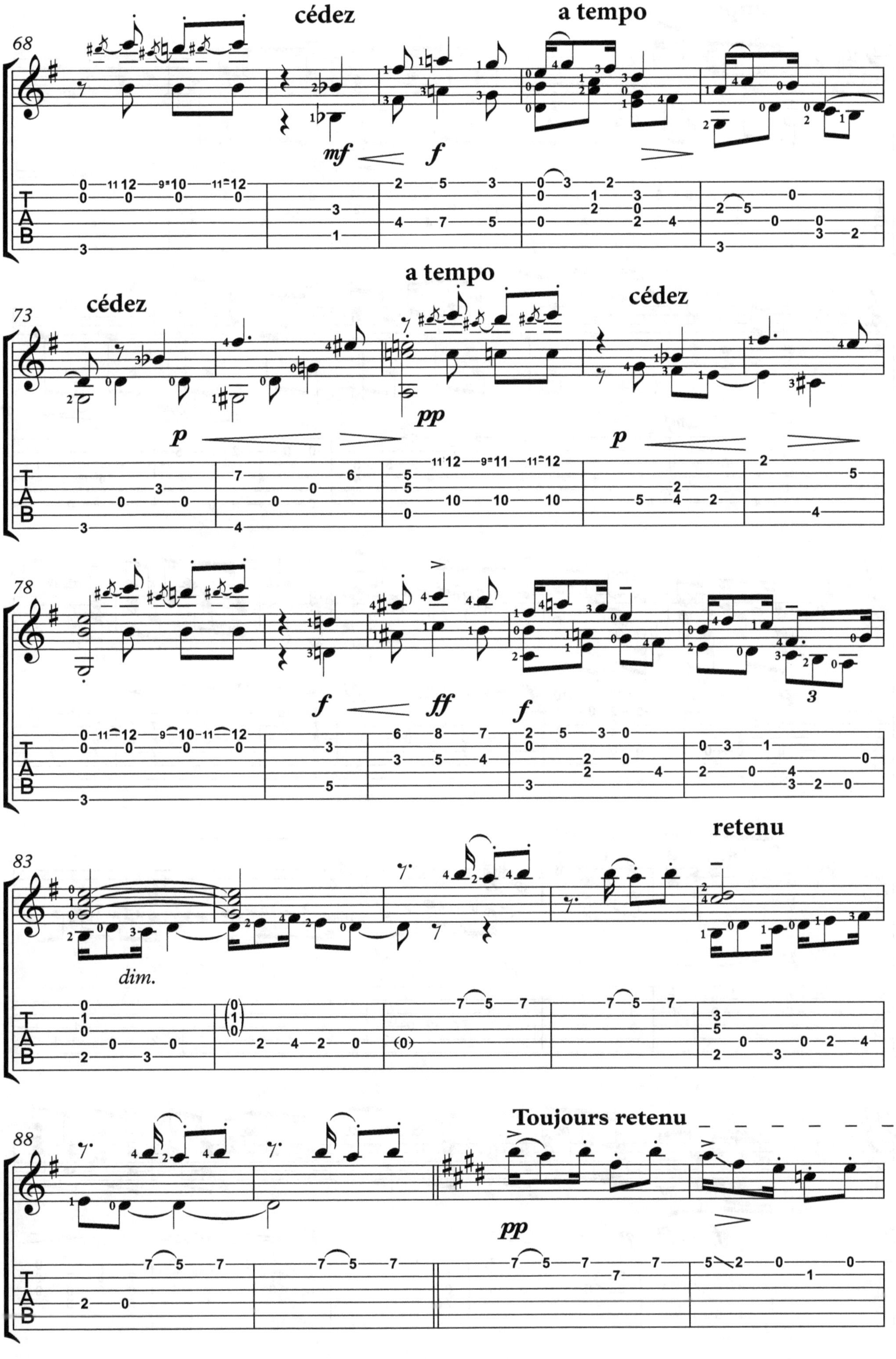
cédez
a tempo
a tempo
cédez
cédez
retenu
dim.
Toujours retenu

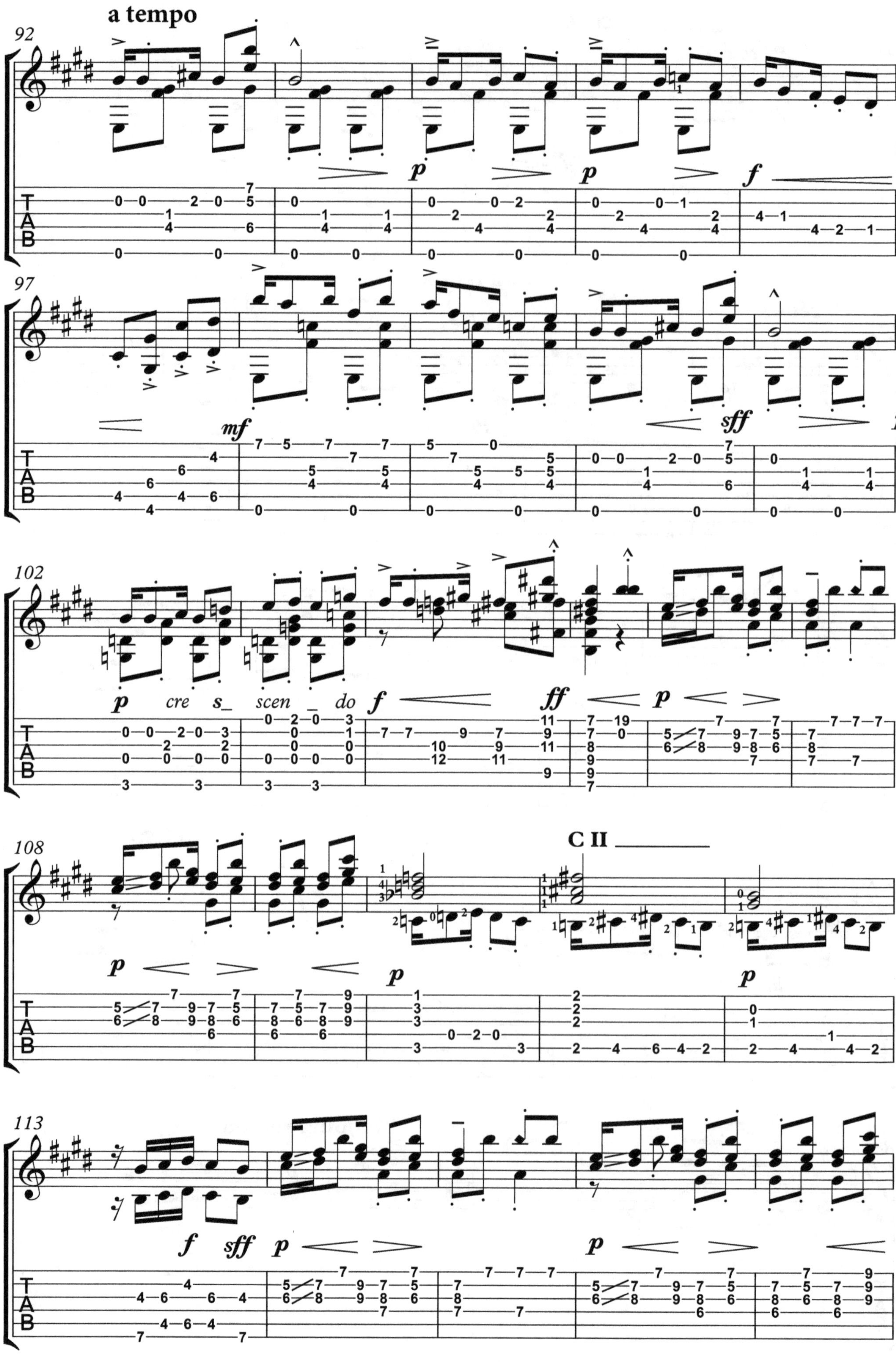
a tempo
92
97
102
cre s_ scen _ do
108
C II
113

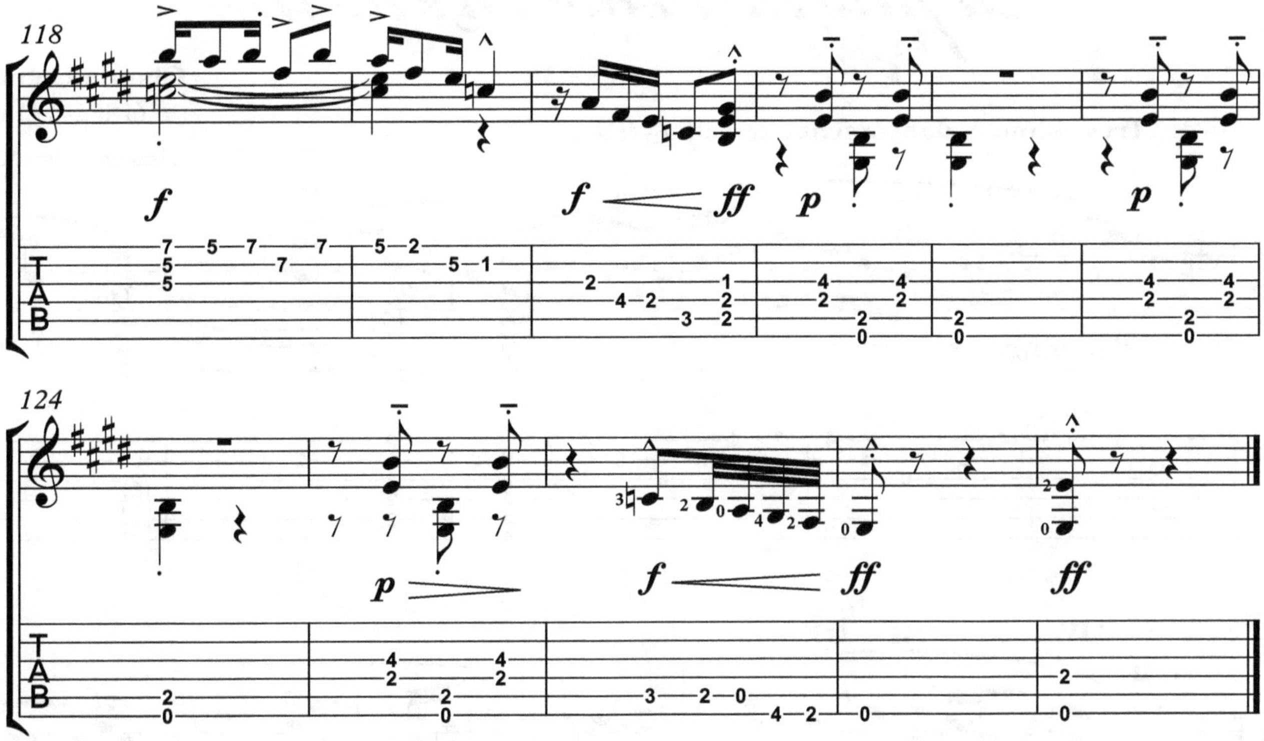
118
124

La fille aux cheveux de lin

Claude Debussy
(1862-1918)

Arranger -Yago Santos

Tres calme et doncement exressif ♩=66

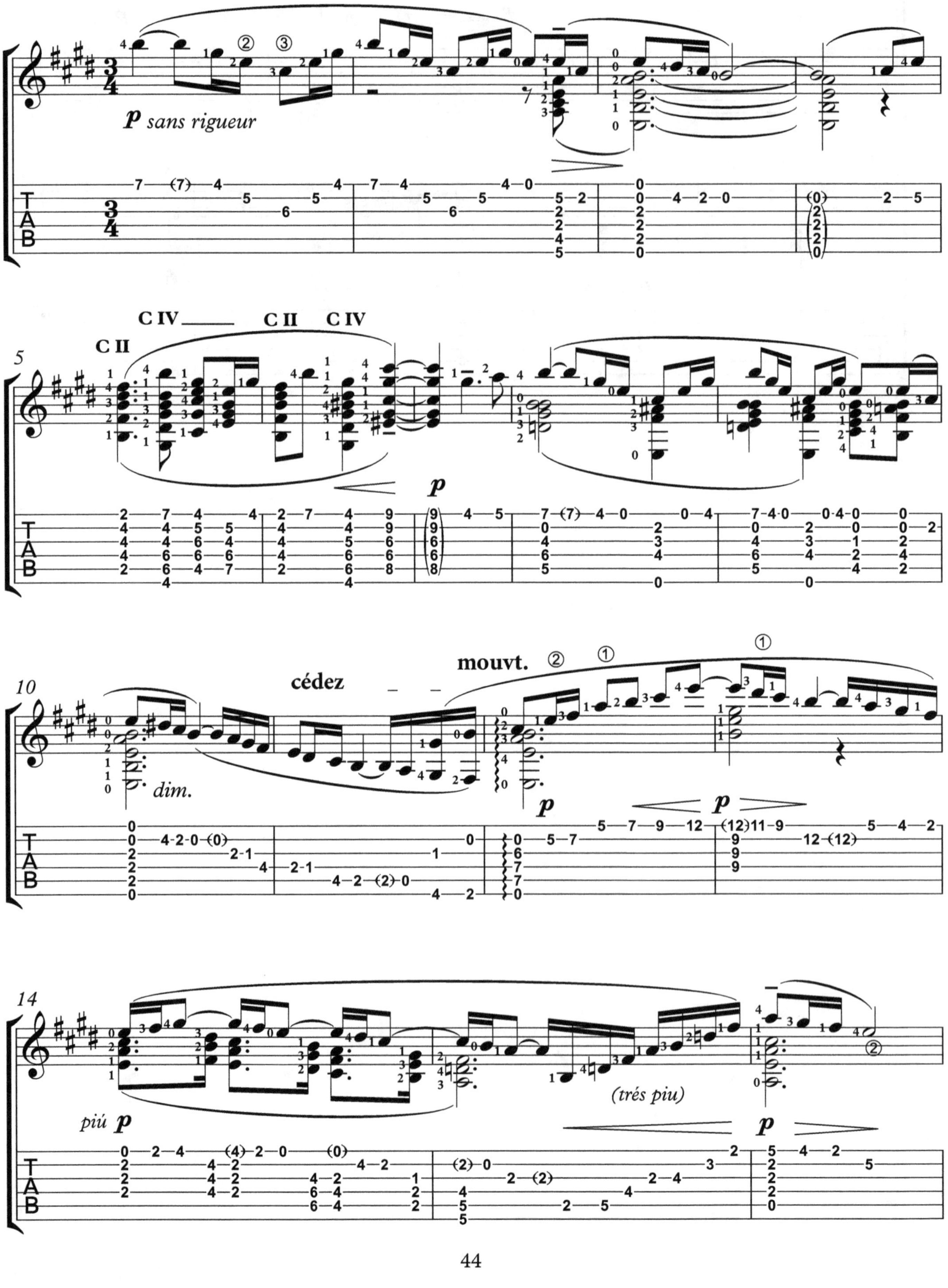

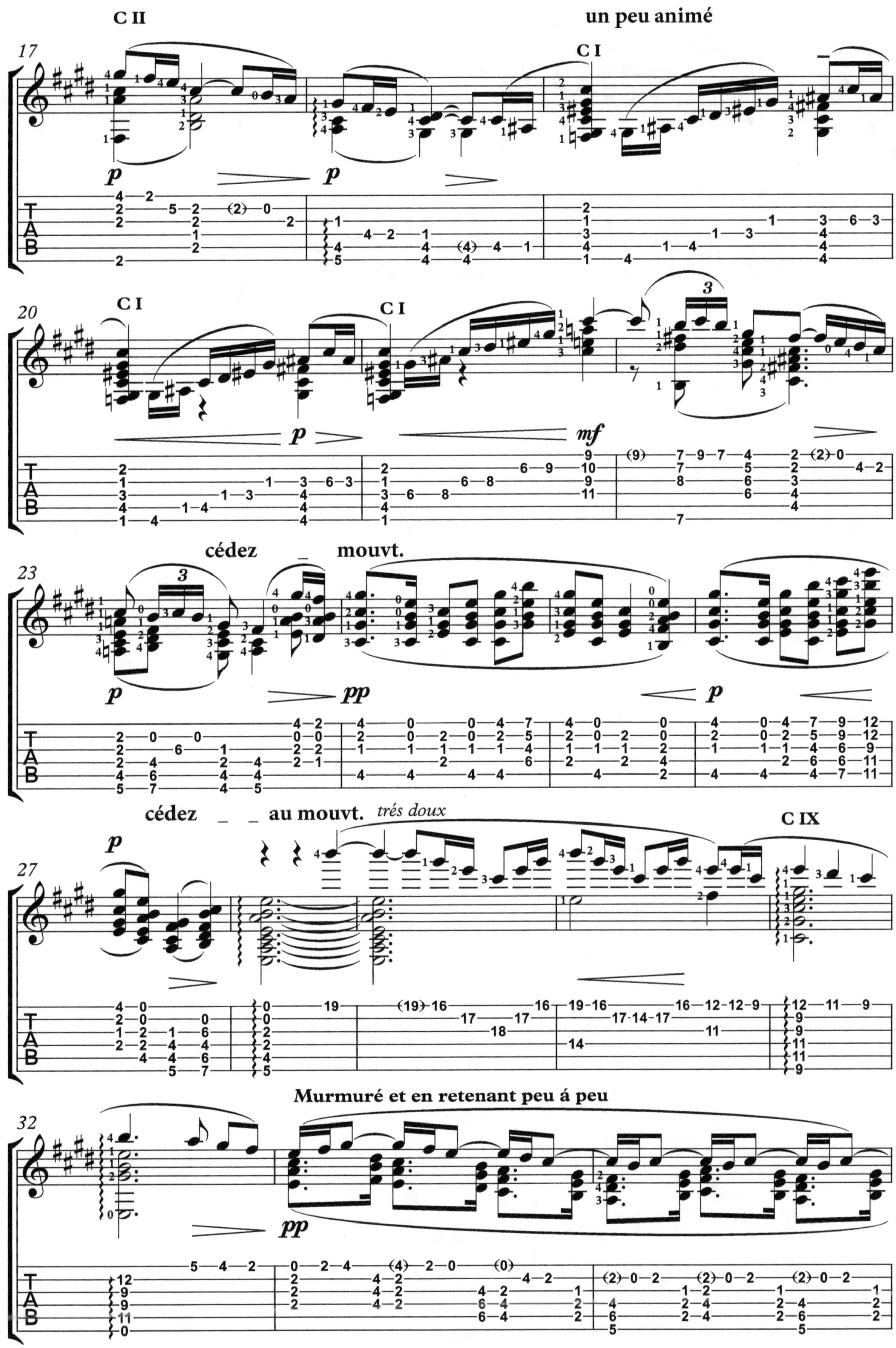
C II
un peu animé
C I
C I
C I
cédez
mouvt.
cédez
au mouvt.
trés doux
C IX
Murmuré et en retenant peu á peu

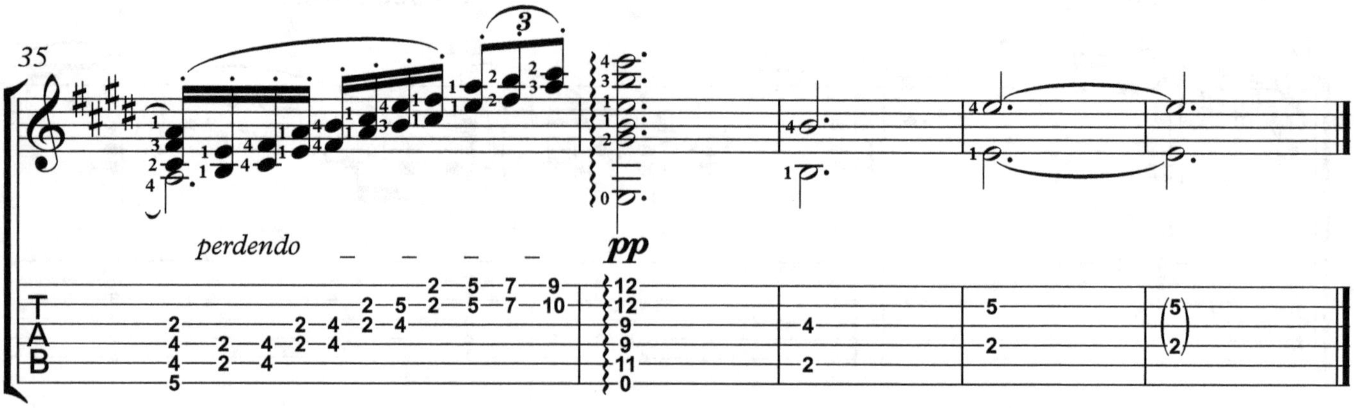
35
perdendo
pp

This page has been left blank to avoid an awkward page turn.

Minstrels

Claude Debussy
(1862-1918)

⑥ — D

Arranger - Yago Santos

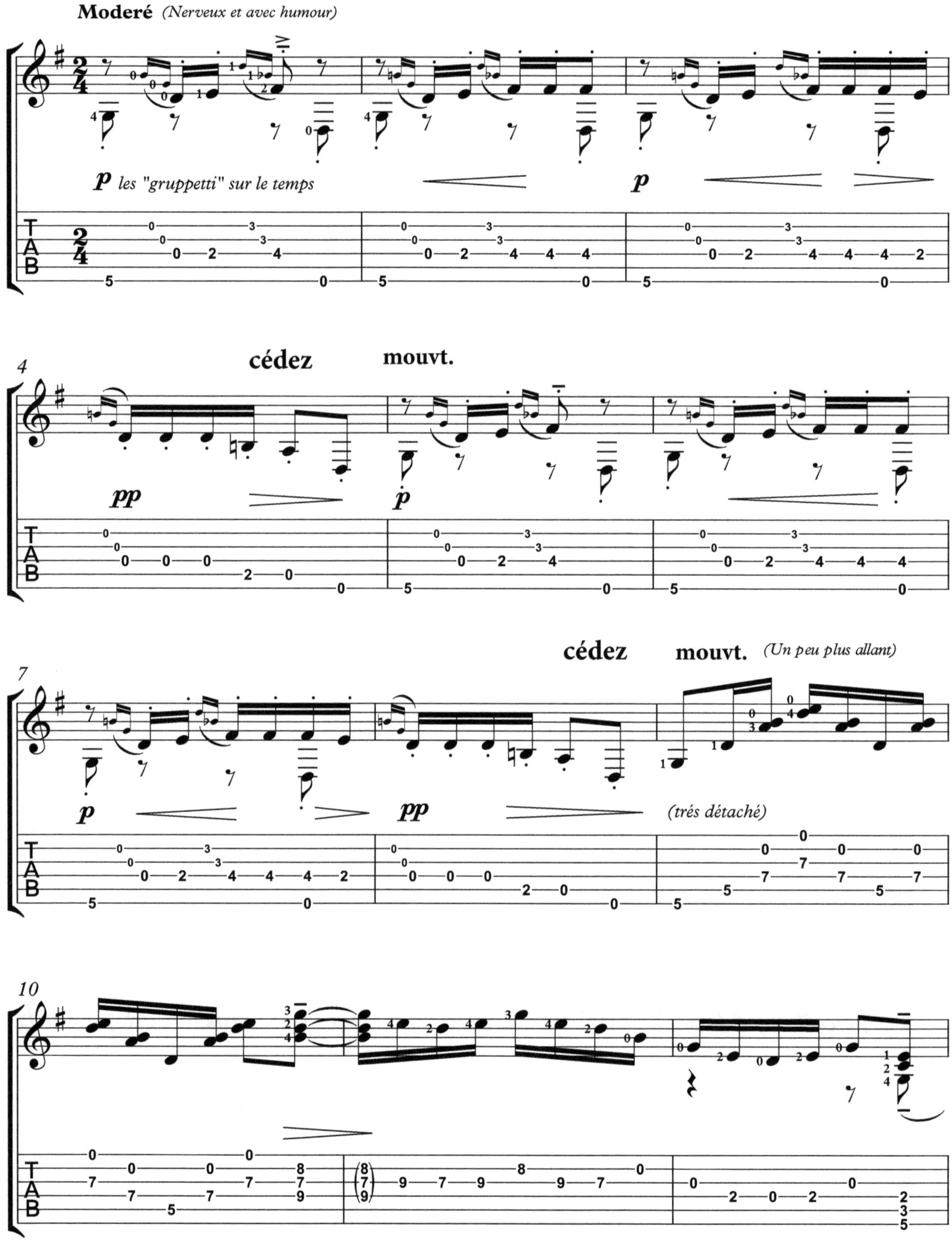

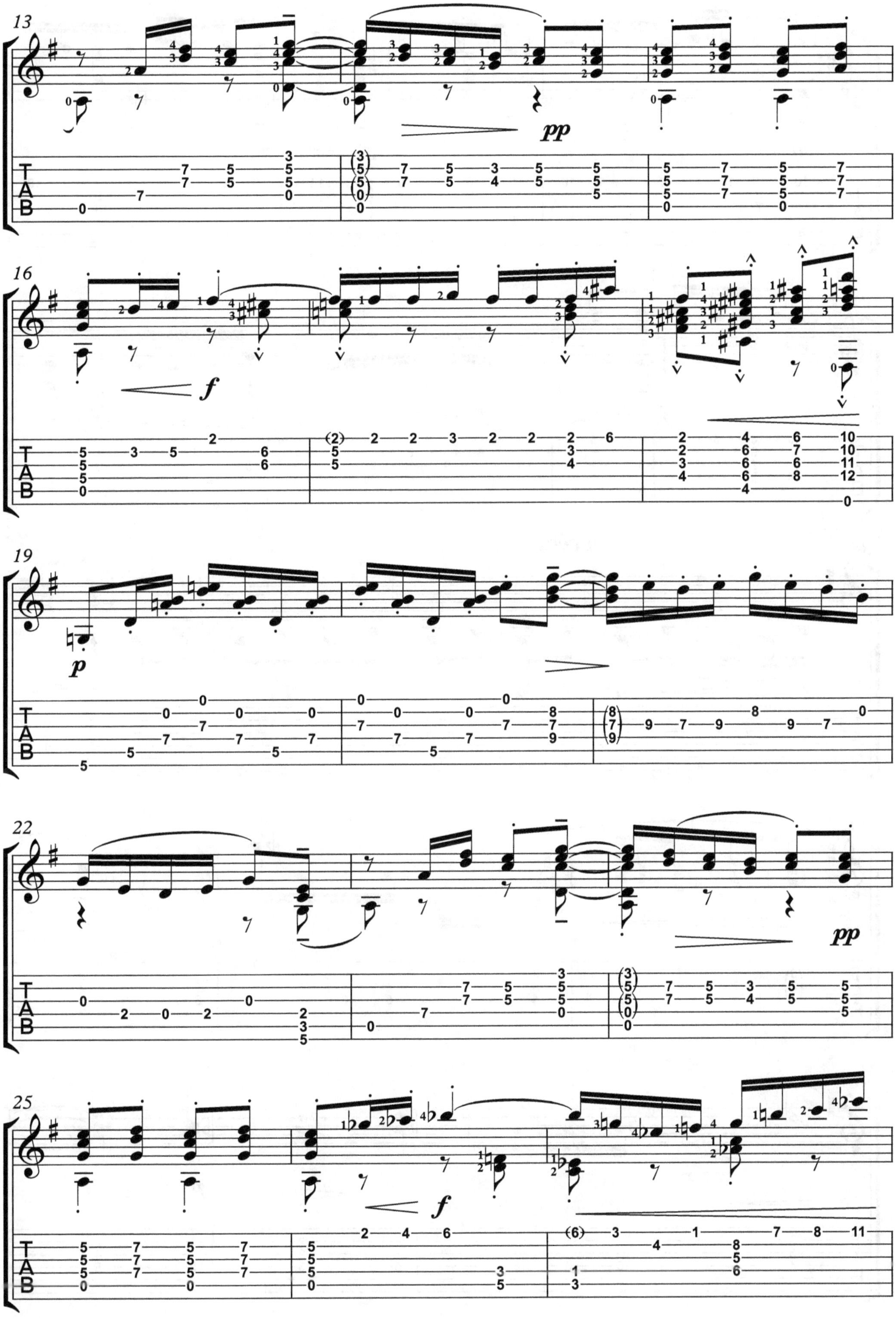

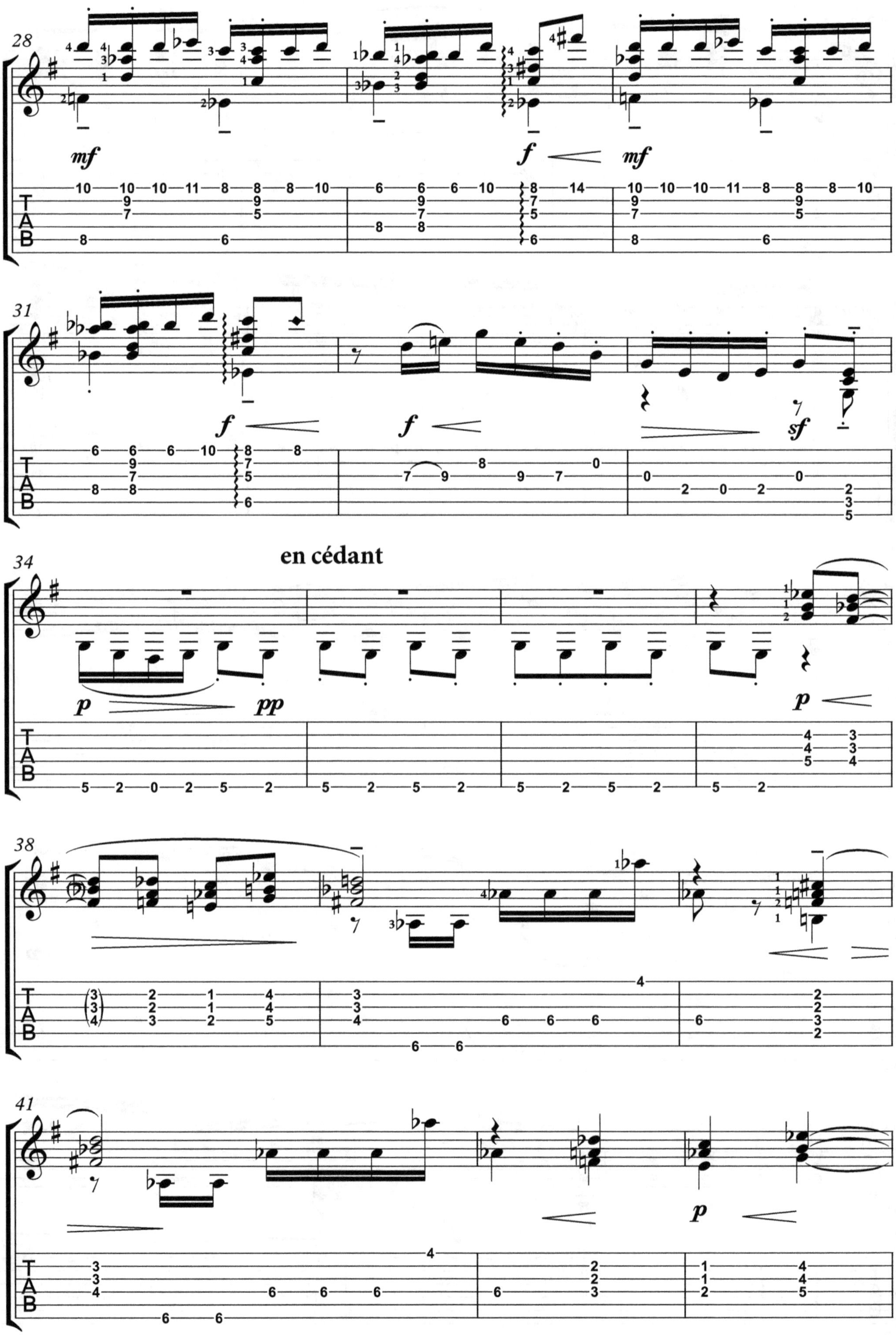
en cédant

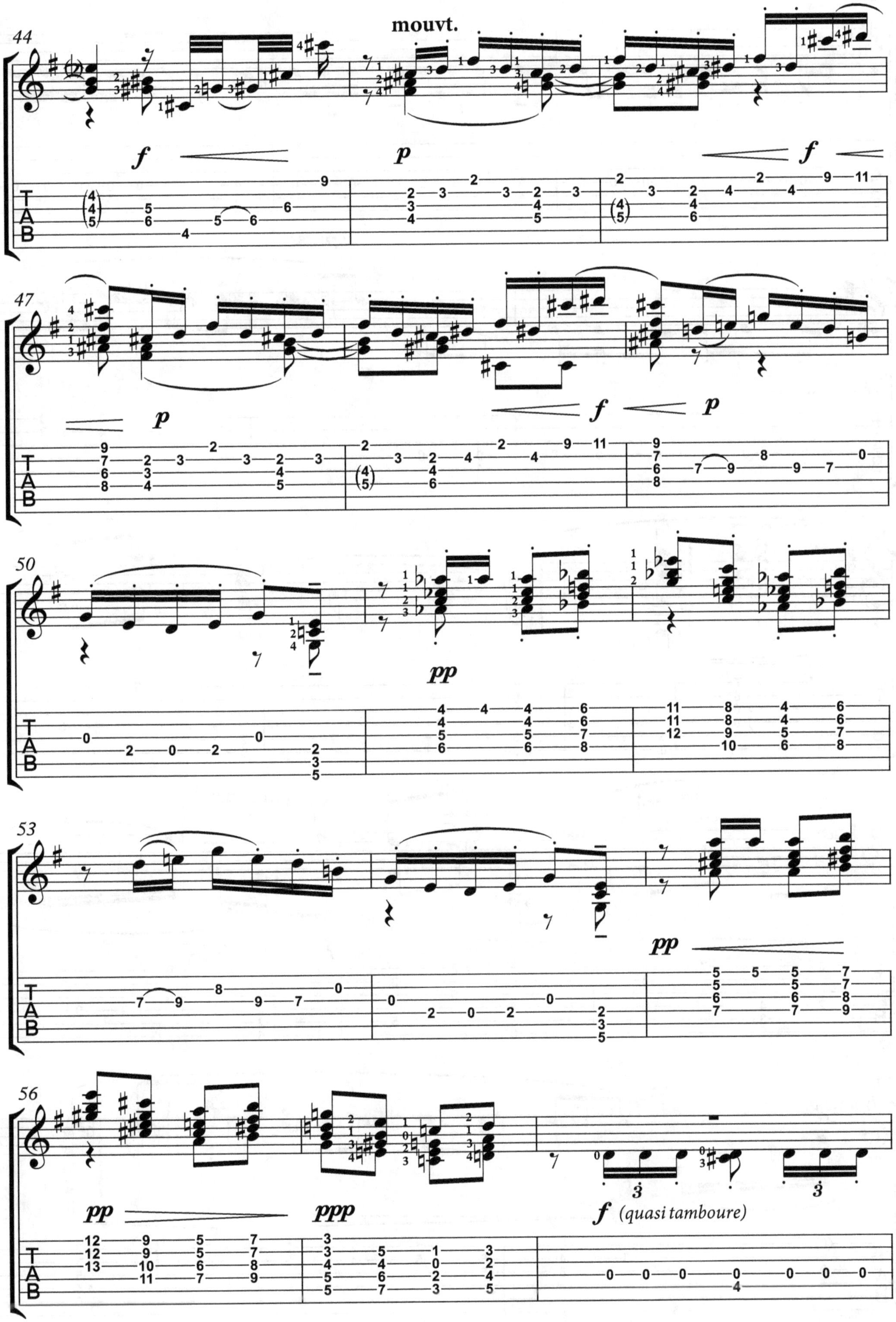
mouvt.
(quasi tamboure)

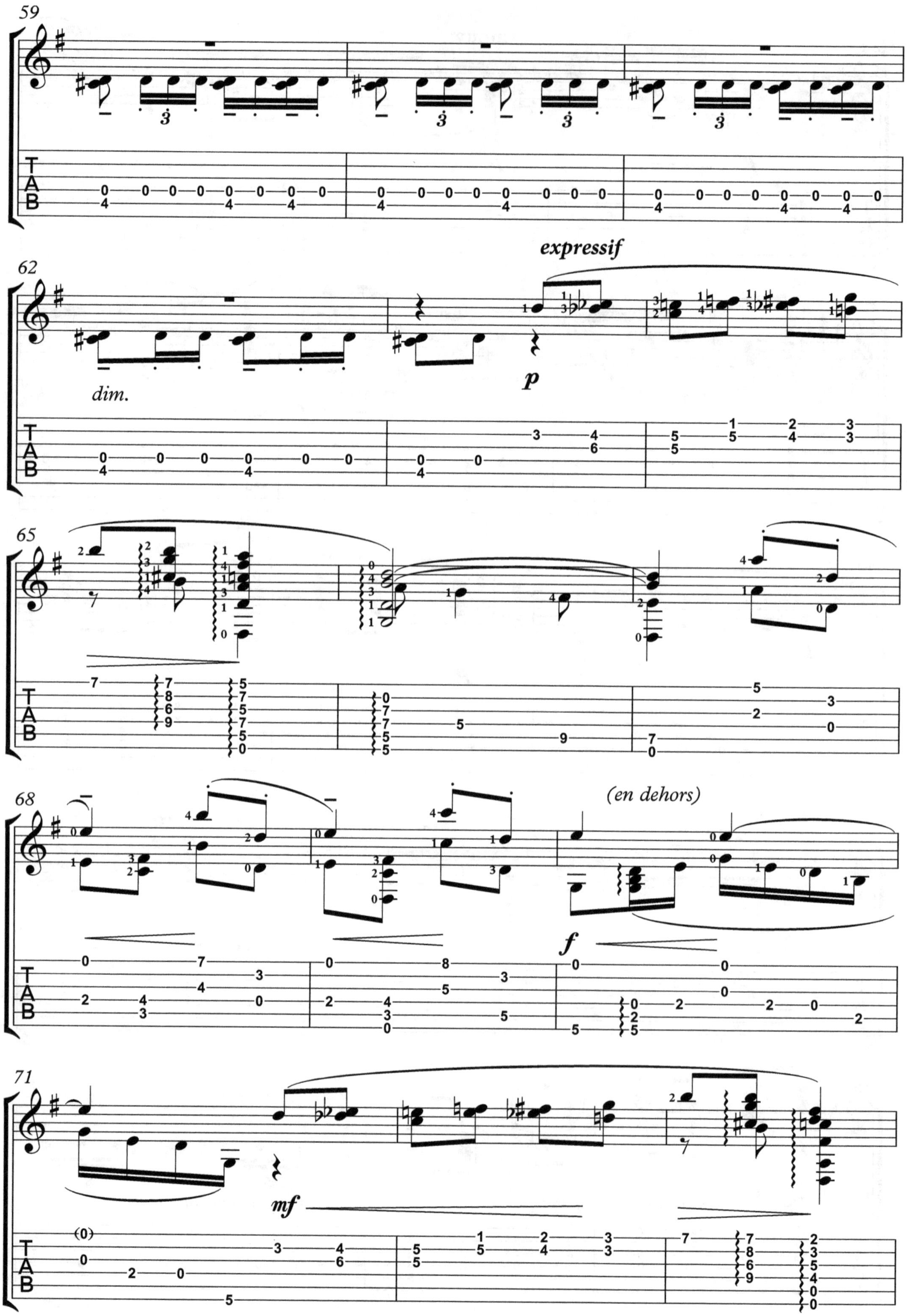
59
62
expressif
dim.
p
65
68
(en dehors)
f
71
mf

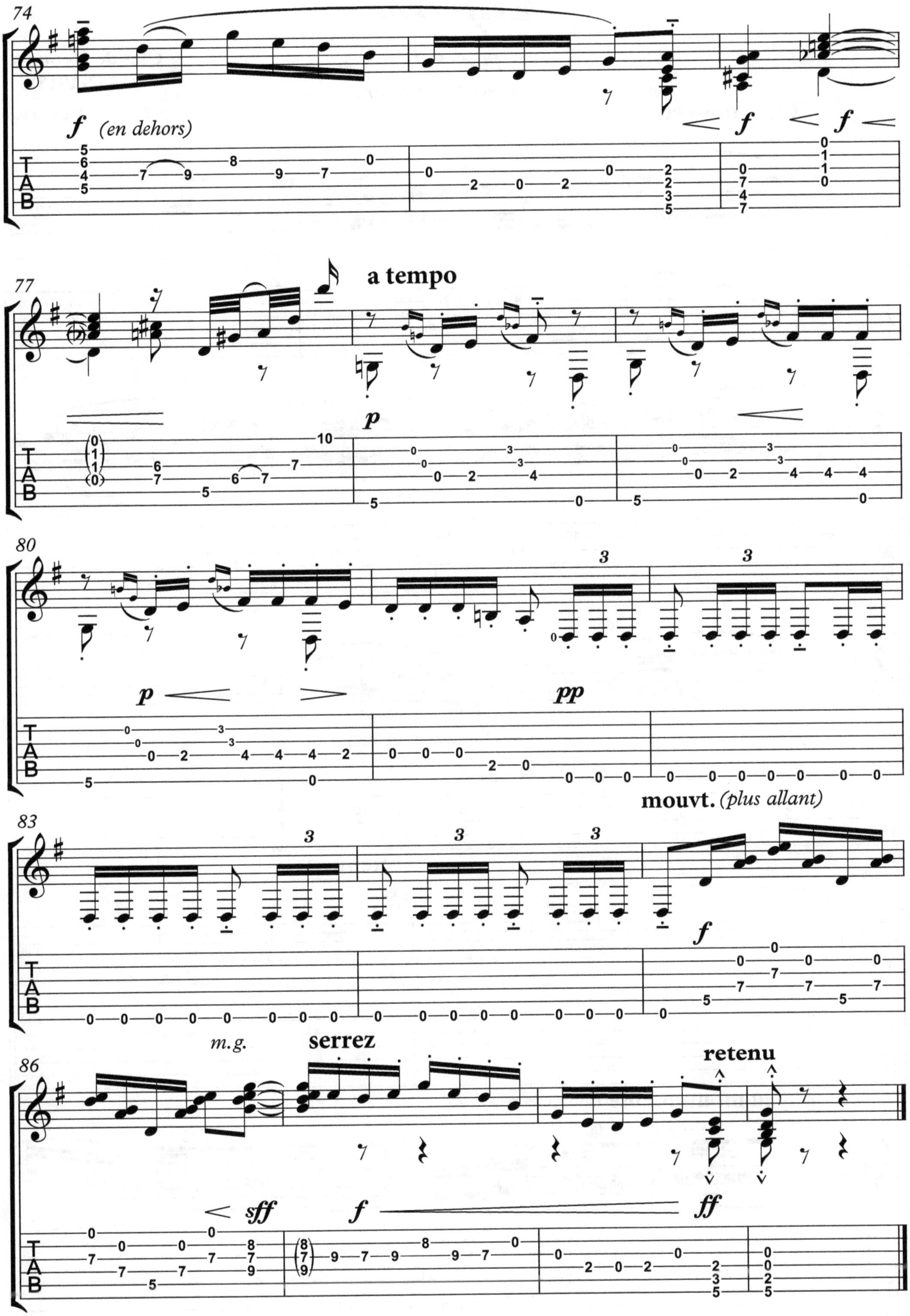
(en dehors)
a tempo
mouvt. (plus allant)
m.g.
serrez
retenu

Syrinx

Flute Solo
Arranged for Guitar

Claude Debussy
(1862-1918)

Arranger - Yago Santos

Tres modéré

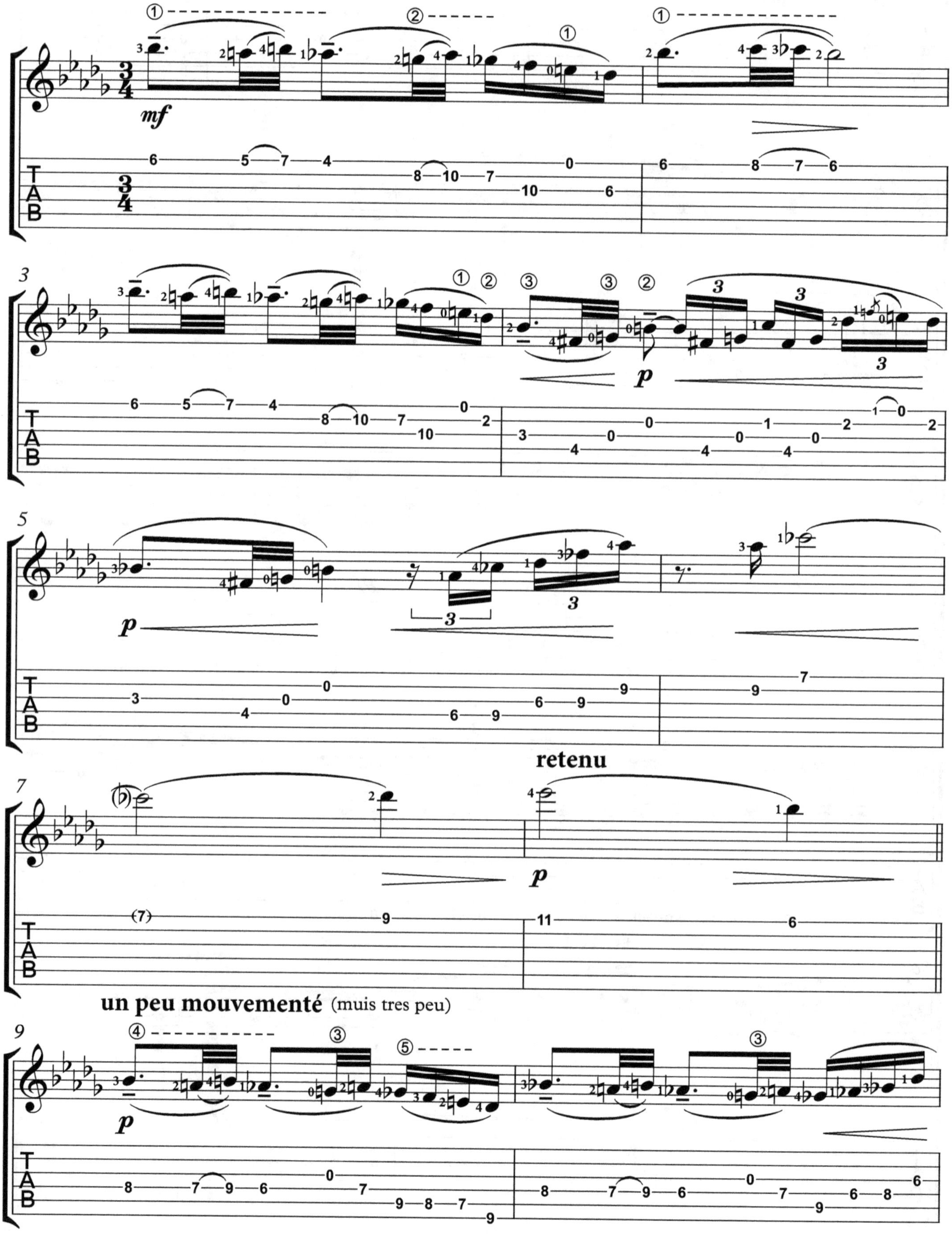

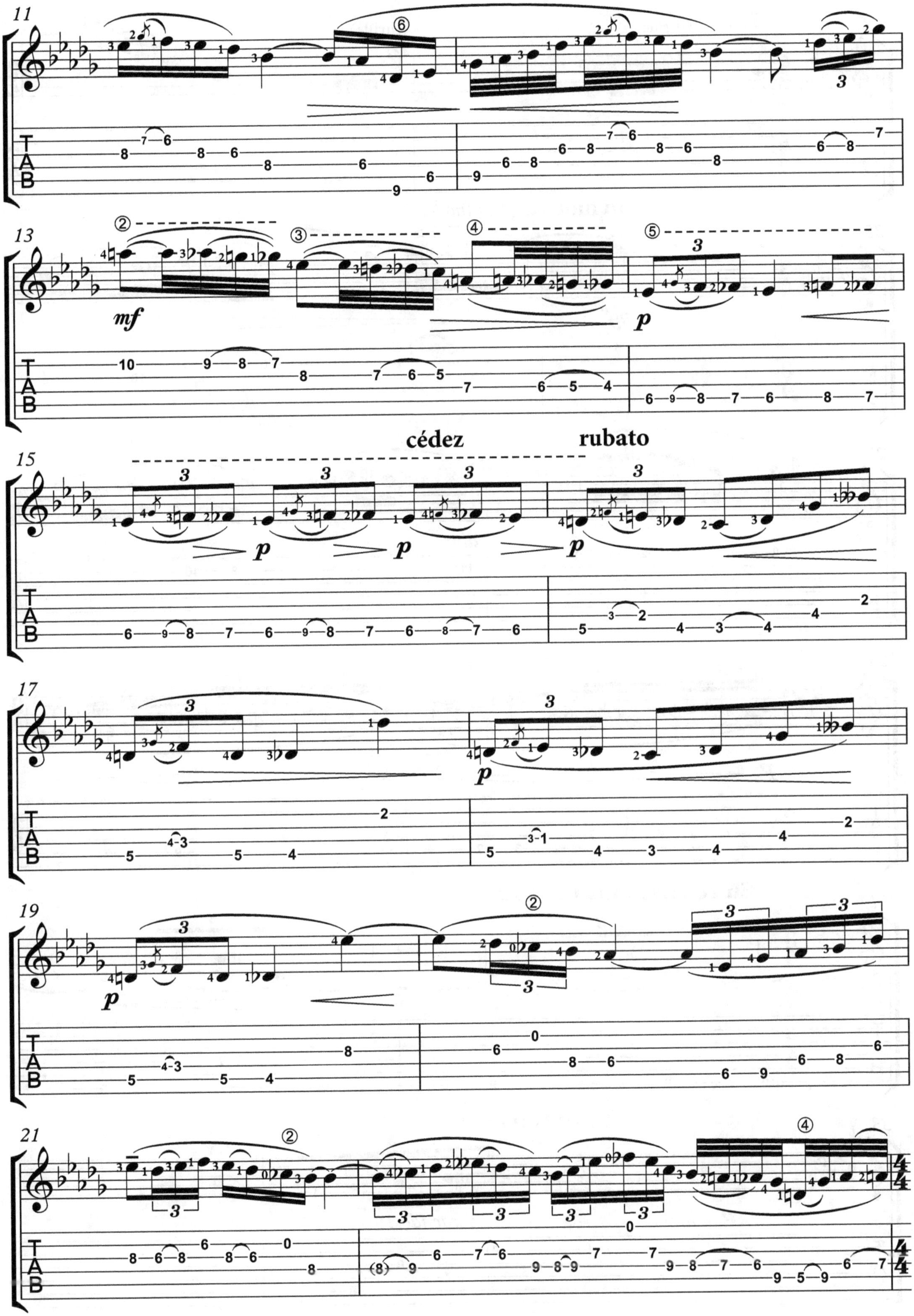
11
13
mf
p
cédez
rubato
15
17
19
21

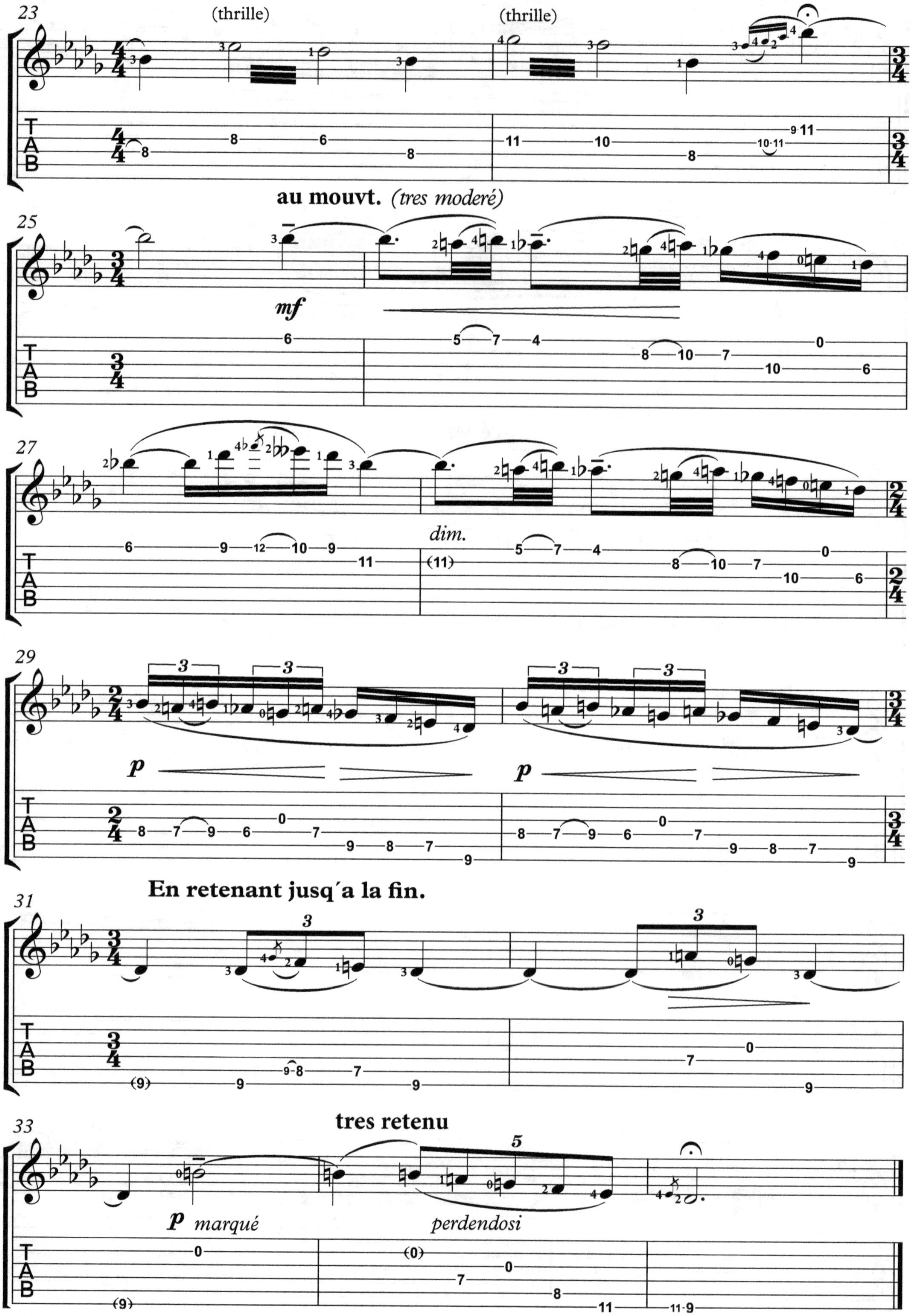
(thrille)
(thrille)
au mouvt. (tres moderé)
mf
dim.
p
p
En retenant jusq´a la fin.
tres retenu
p marqué
perdendosi

Le petit nègre

Claude Debussy
(1862-1918)

Arranger - Yago Santos

Allegro giusto

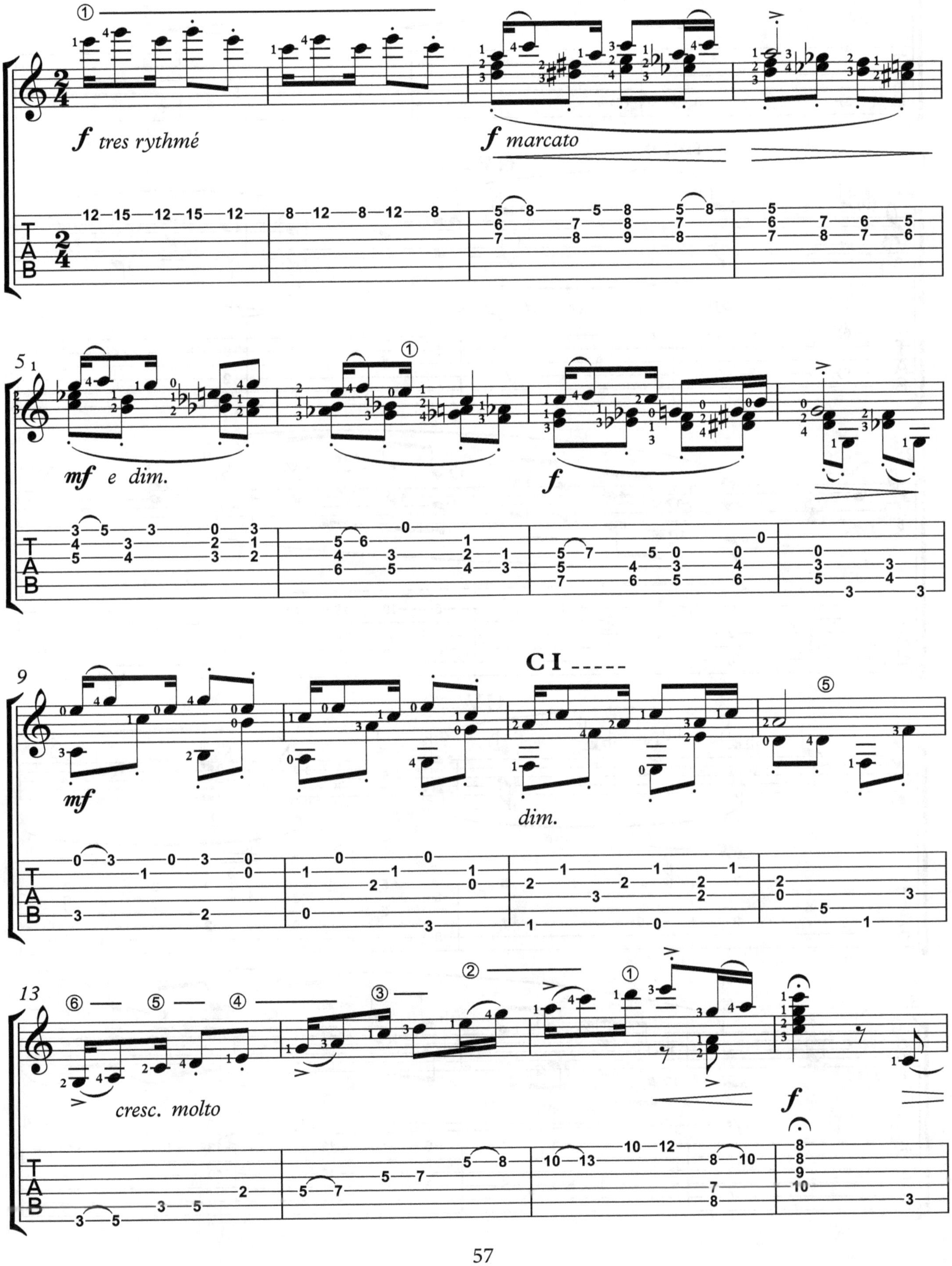

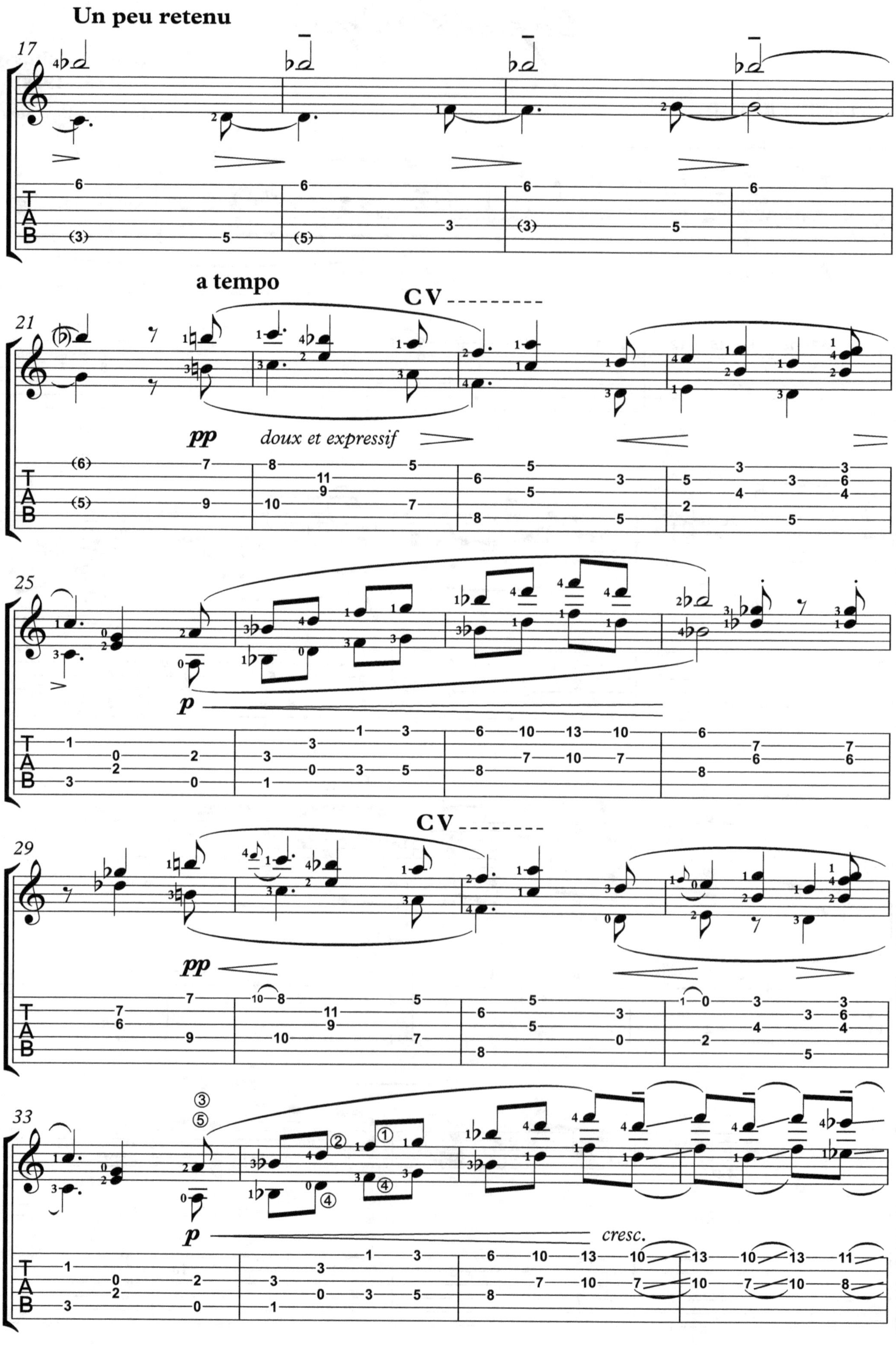
Un peu retenu
a tempo
CV
pp
doux et expressif
p
CV
pp
p
cresc.

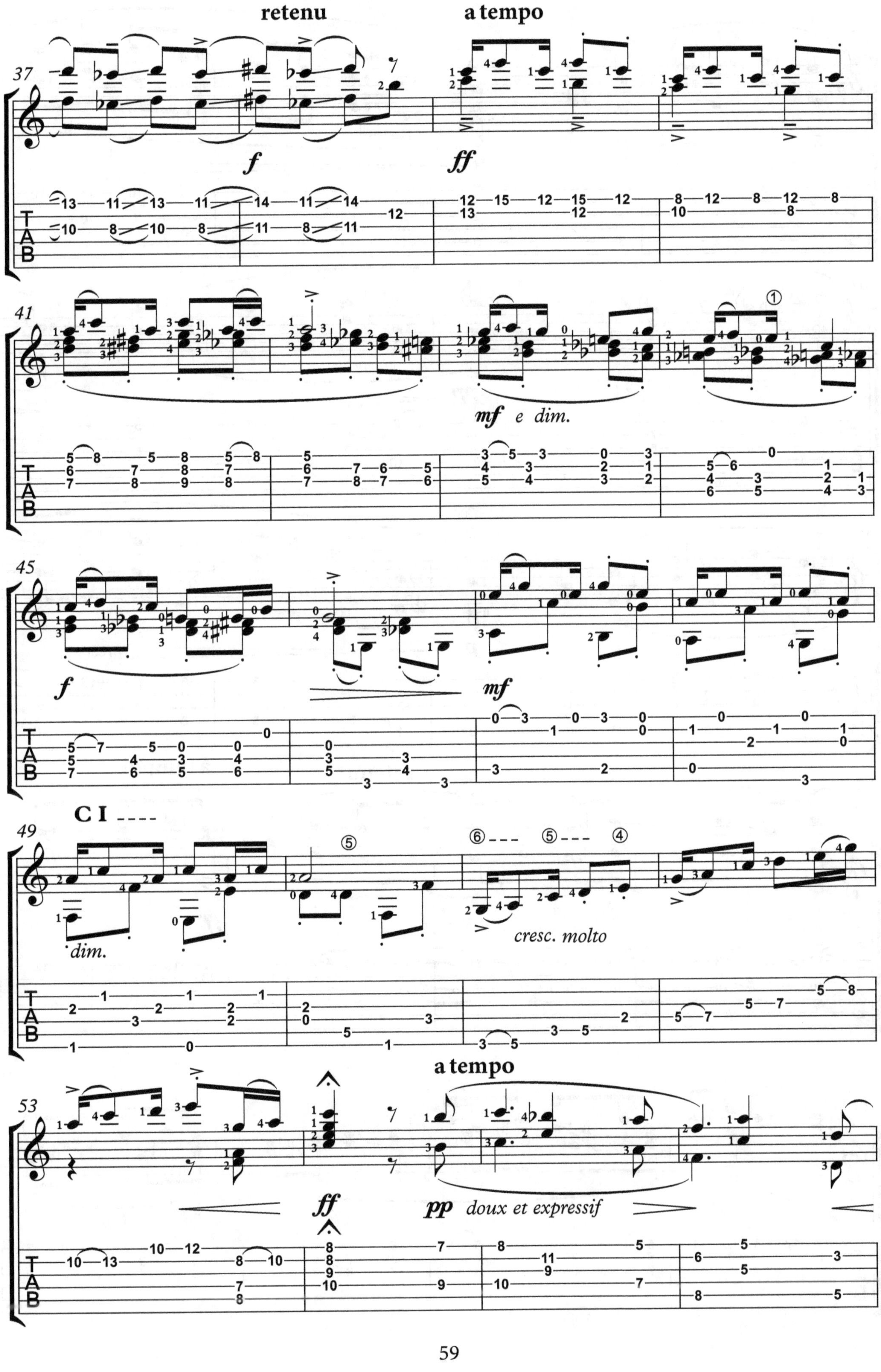
retenu
a tempo
f
ff
mf e dim.
f
mf
C I
dim.
cresc. molto
a tempo
ff
pp doux et expressif

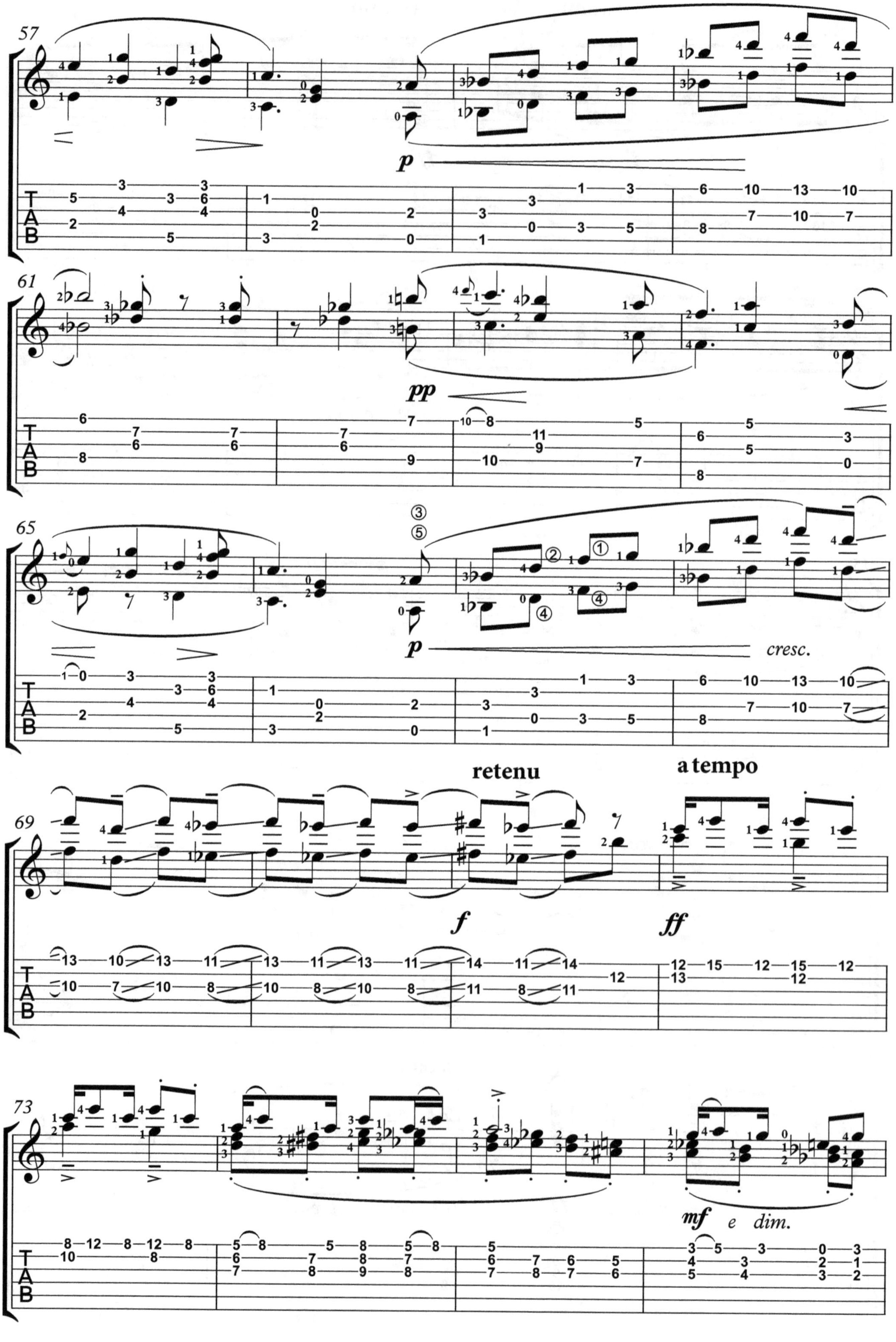
57
61
65
69
73
cresc.
retenu
a tempo
e dim.

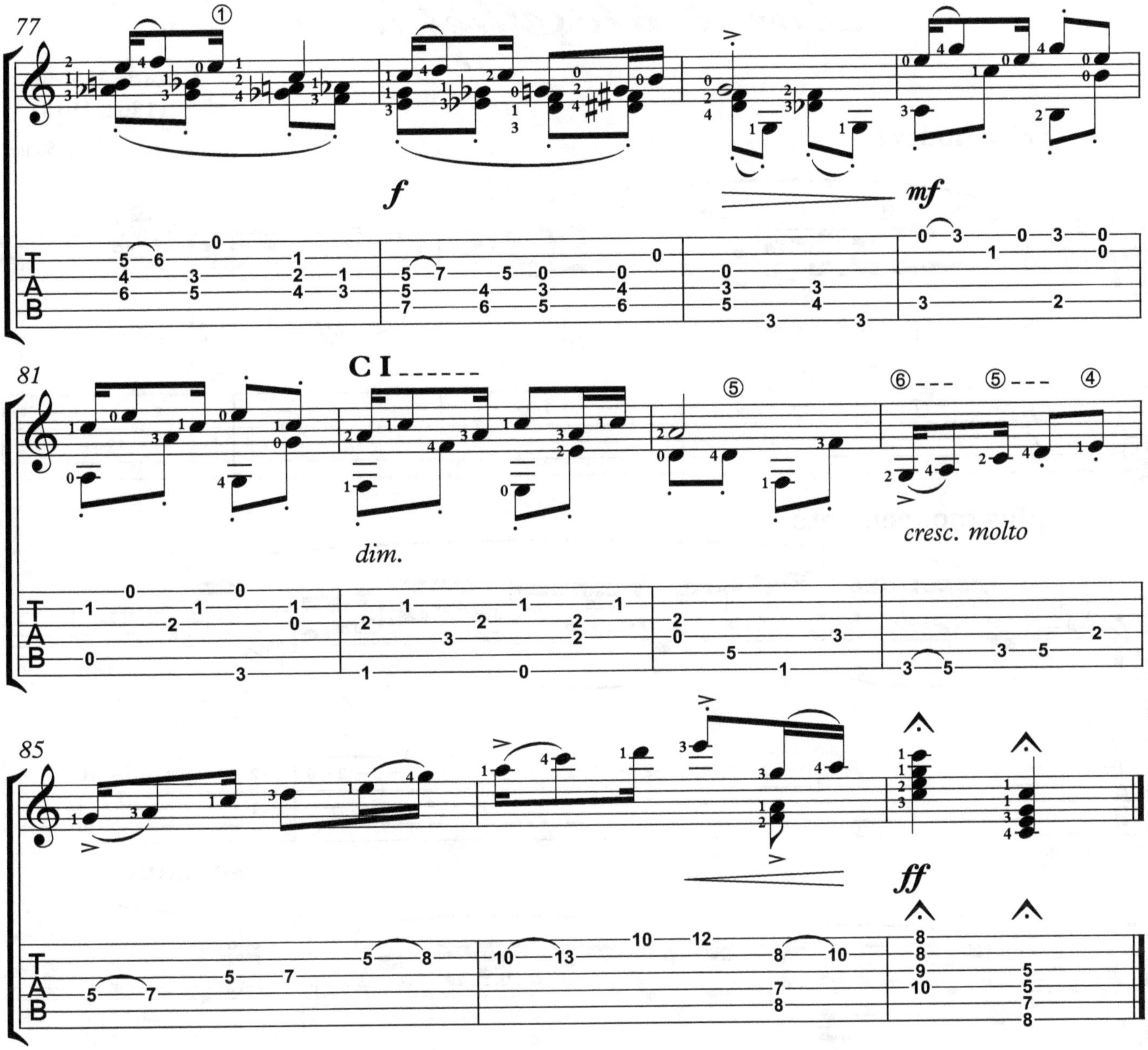
77
f
mf
81
C I
dim.
cresc. molto
85
ff

The Little Shepherd

Claude Debussy
(1862-1918)

Arranger - Yago Santos

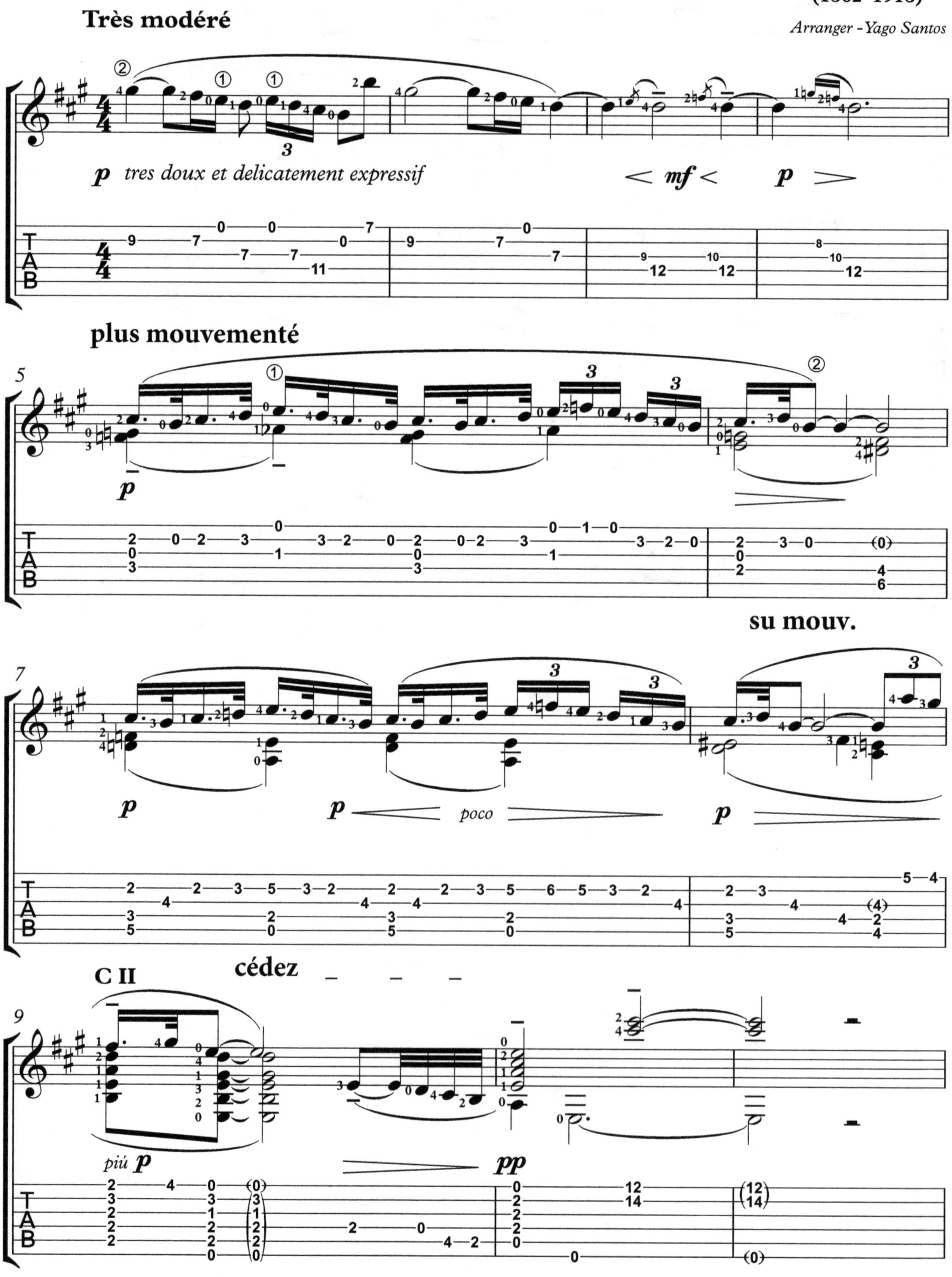

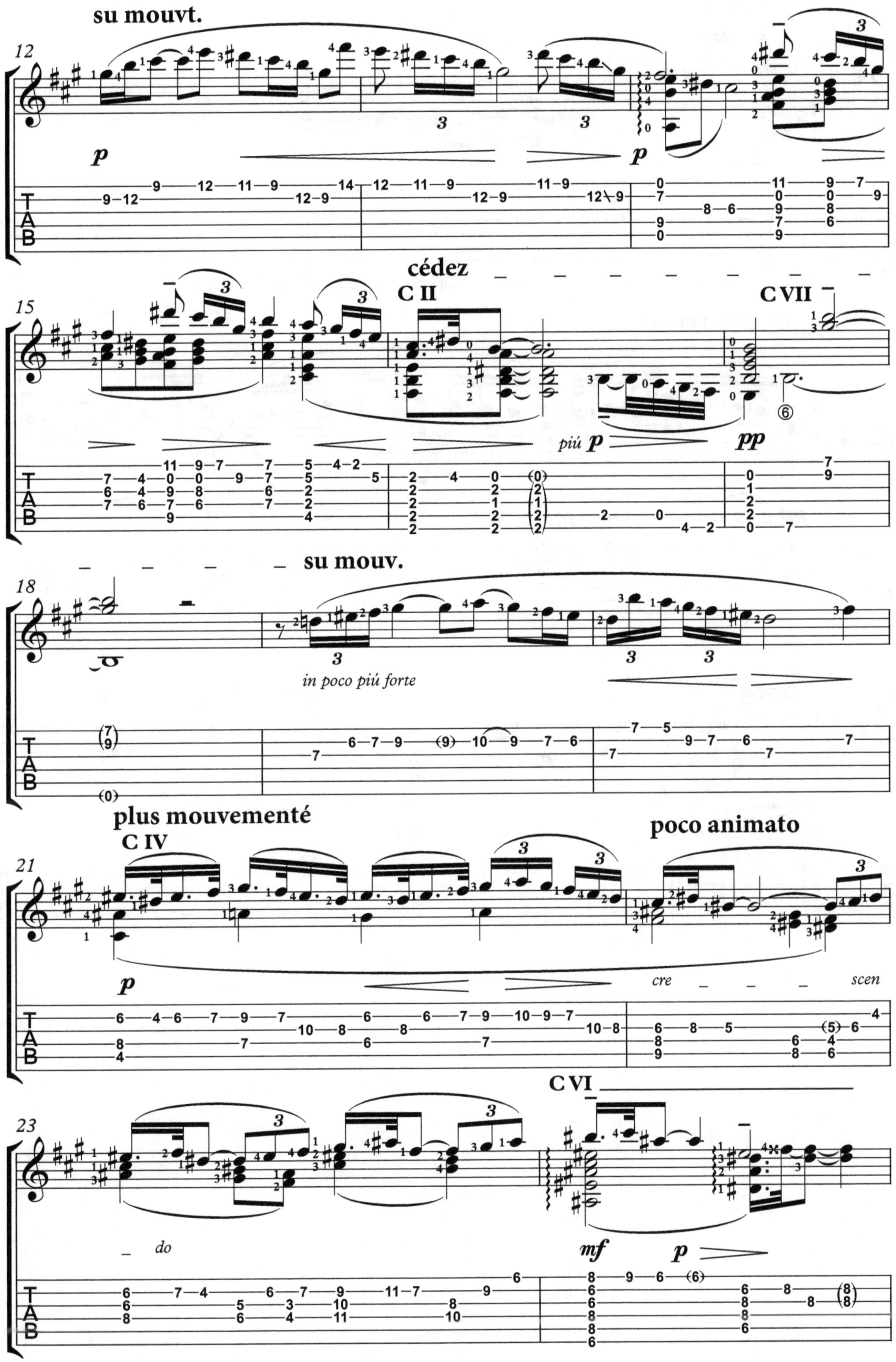
su mouvt.
cédez
C II
C VII
piú p
pp
su mouv.
in poco piú forte
plus mouvementé
C IV
poco animato
cre
scen
do
C VI
mf

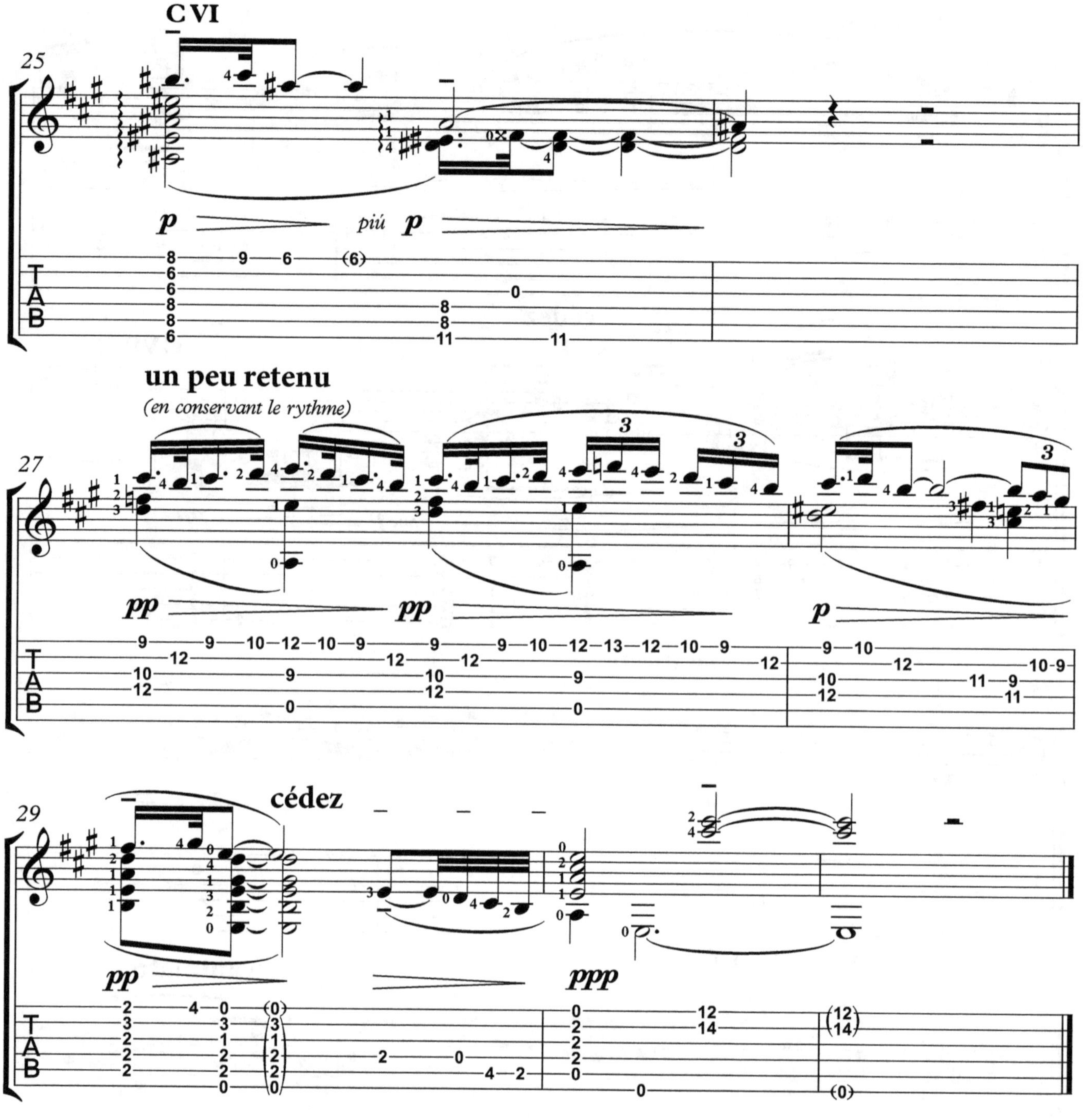
C VI
piú p
un peu retenu
(en conservant le rythme)
cédez